The Liturgy of Liberation

The Confession and Forgiveness of Sins

THEODORE W. JENNINGS, Jr.

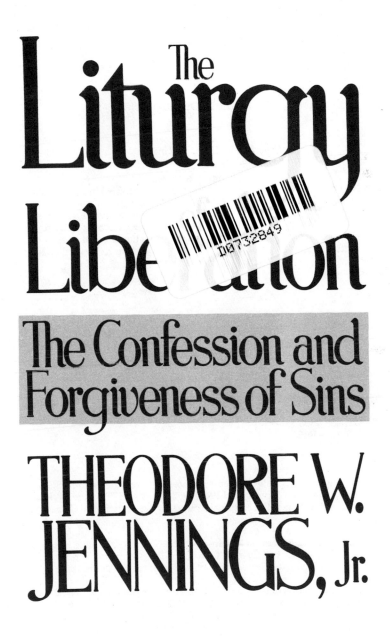

Abingdon Press
Nashville

For Helen and Theo Kotze

THE LITURGY OF LIBERATION

Library of Congress Cataloging-in-Publication Data

Jennings, Theodore W.
  The liturgy of liberation: the confession and forgiveness of sins/ Theodore W. Jennings, Jr.
  p. cm.
ISBN 0-687-22172-2 (alk. paper)
  1. Confession (Liturgy) I. Title.
BV845.J43 1988
  265'.62—dc19

87-19828
CIP

Scripture quotations unless otherwise noted are from the Revised Standard Version of the Bible, copyrighted 1946, 1952, © 1971, 1973, by the Division of Christian Education of the National Council of the Churches of Christ in the U.S.A., and used by permission.

Scripture quotations noted NEB are from the New English Bible. Copyright © the Delegates of the Oxford University Press and the Syndics of the Cambridge University Press 1961, 1970. Reprinted by permission.

Scripture quotations designated GNB are from the *Good News Bible*, the Bible in Today's English Version. Copyright © American Bible Society, 1976.

MANUFACTURED BY THE PARTHENON PRESS AT
NASHVILLE, TENNESSEE, UNITED STATES OF AMERICA

Preface

When we gather as the community of faith we confess our sins and hear spoken the divine word of forgiveness. Is this merely an incidental act in our worship, or is it something of fundamental importance not only for our worship but also for our everyday lives as followers of Jesus? In this book I try to show that this action we perform in church is a pattern for our life in the world. This work is therefore a continuation of my reflections on the worship of the church as the key to an understanding of Christian life and witness begun in *Life as Worship: Prayer and Praise in Jesus' Name* (1982). Both the earlier study of prayer and praise and the present reflection on the confession and forgiveness of sins aim at a theology for the church based on the central actions of the church's life.

I first became convinced of the necessity for and the possibility of such a theology for the church during a visit some years ago with the Christian Institute of South Africa. The struggle of the church in that troubled land to speak a compelling word of witness to the gospel of truth, freedom, and reconciliation made clear that theology could not be an idle academic exercise but must seek to be of concrete service to the witness of the church. The sense of the importance of this task has grown as my wife and I have worked as missionaries with the church in Mexico and with

Christians from the tortured lands of Central America.

Yet these reflections are not addressed to the Christian communities of Africa and Latin America so much as to those of the "first world," which is my home. This book grows out of a study for laity in the Palo Alto United Methodist Church, which I led under the auspices of the Trinity Center of Berkeley, California. Thus from its beginning this book has been directed toward the actual life of the church and of ordinary Christians in North America.

When I was writing the first draft of this work my wife and I were host to a loved one who was passing through the dark and terrifying night of mental illness. We were also deeply concerned about the fate of friends imprisoned or banned in South Africa. Thus intra-psychic and sociopolitical brokenness constitute twin themes in these reflections on the liberation for which we hope and that we enact together in the confession and forgiveness of sins.

In a world so dominated as is ours by the signs of bondage to the law of sin and death, it is not easy to rely on the liberating power of the gospel of truth. I would not have the courage to write of liberation were the gospel not made flesh and blood in the lives of those I know and love. I am grateful to this cloud of witnesses from many lands and walks of life. These include Ronna Case, who as companion in marriage and colleague in ministry speaks the truth in love, and the friends we met in the Christian Institute of South Africa who are witnesses to the gospel of liberation. This book is dedicated to two of these friends, whose lives demonstrate the word of Paul: Where the Spirit is, there is freedom.

Contents

PART ONE

Foundations

Introduction

1

A. Theology and the Church

W hat does theology have to do with the church? This question is a perplexing one for North American Protestants. In other parts of the universal church, theology is typically understood as a necessary function of the church's life, but this no longer appears true for us. Indeed a gulf of mutual suspicion and even antagonism seems to separate the work of systematic and constructive theology from the institutions and corporate life of denominations and communities of faith.

The strong pragmatic orientation of North American culture permeates the life of the churches and their strong emphasis on programs for extending, preserving, and adding vitality to church life. This activism succeeds in retaining the loyalty of large sectors of the population, but it also encounters the perennial risk of substituting loyalty to the church for commitment to the gospel. Often Christian identity is little more than identification with the dominant values of the culture as a whole, and an acceptable amount of participation in the church as a voluntary association.

At the same time, theology has found its home in the academic institutions of our society rather than in the church. Systematic or constructive theology is preoccupied with the attempt to build bridges to other disciplines in the university and so to defend its academic status. The result is a concentration of theological energy on the rather arcane questions of theological method and the turn from constructive to historical studies.[1]

It is little wonder, in this environment, that even leaders of the churches trained in schools of theology may ask, What does theology have to do with the church?

The result of this malaise is that theology as a reflection on the basic character of Christian faith seems nearly to have disappeared, while the community of faith takes on the character of a voluntary association whose Christian identity is simply assumed but seldom made evident. Theology appears sterile. The church appears barren. Both have become preoccupied, gazing at themselves in a mirror—turned inward. Both have lost their principal theme—the identity and meaning of the Christian faith.

Since earliest times the fate of the church has been tied to the fate of theology. Where one loses its power the other fades. We do not have to return to the first five centuries of the Christian community with its rapid expansion and astonishing theological vitality to see this connection. We do not even have to return to the Reformation with its renewal of church life on the basis of a theological renaissance. We can learn the same lesson from our own century.

The astonishing vigor of theology in Europe in the first half of this century emerged in response to the debacle of the First World War and the rise of fascism. This situation confronted the church with the question of its identity. Does the church perish with the collapse of the nineteenth-century civilization? Is Christian faith compatible with the rise of the totalitarian state? The response was to construct a theology directed toward

---

1. This theme is elaborated in my introductory essay to *The Vocation of the Theologian*, ed. Theodore W. Jennings, Jr. (Philadelphia: Fortress Press, 1985).

the practice of the church in proclamation and witness. Thus the theologies of Barth, Brunner, Bonhoeffer, and Bultmann were, above all, theologies for preaching. They were theologies that sought to serve the proclamation of the church through a critical reflection on the foundation, the fidelity, and the goal of preaching.

Something similar has happened in the Christian communities of the Third World. There too the identity of the Christian community has been seriously questioned. Is Christianity an alien European religion, or can it be genuinely African, Asian, or Latin? Is Christianity the religion of the colonial powers, of the imperialists, of the exploiters, of the rich? Or is it as well or instead the faith of the poor and the power of liberation? The life of faith in these parts of the world is at stake in these questions. And where the question of Christian identity is taken seriously we see as well an increasingly vigorous theology: the liberation theology of Latin America, Africa, and Asia. The vitality of the community and the vigor of theology are closely intertwined.

What do these examples of the marriage of theology and the life of the church, taken from situations quite different from our own, have to teach us in mainline American middle-class Protestant churches?

Only by way of serious attention to the identity, the life, the actual practice of the Christian community can theology once again become a meaningful and vigorous discipline. Only by way of a critical reflection on the basis and aim of its practice, and its life, can the church acquire a compelling sense of its identity and mission.

This will also mean that some paths are closed to us. It will not do for theologians simply to inform the church concerning the latest results of theological work. This way would presume that the current work of theology is the norm or standard to which the life of the community of faith must conform.

But a theological reflection that is not oriented toward the community of faith can only appear speculative and irrelevant for that community.

Often when people in the church ask for a more "relevant theology" they appear to mean a language that describes and legitimates what the church is already doing. But this supposes that the church is in no real need of theology, that it already knows perfectly well what it is doing and supposed to do. This would leave the institutional self-preoccupation of the church unchallenged.

Instead of these fruitless paths another must be chosen. The church and theology must attend to the question that addresses them both: How are we to understand our lives in relation to the gospel? Thus we must focus together on the issue of Christian identity, of Christian faithfulness, of Christian mission in the world.

How shall we begin? Where can we begin a fruitful dialogue between theology and the life of the church? I propose that we use as our common starting point something that unites us—the worship of the community.

The church does many things. It builds buildings, recruits members, educates them, mobilizes them, trains them for leadership, studies issues, takes stands on them, and so on. But one thing we always do is worship. We may have no building, few members, no leaders, no Sunday school; but if we gather together in the name of Jesus, we are as much a church as the finest, largest, and busiest church. We come together to pray, to sing praise, to hear the Word of God, to confess our sins, to receive forgiveness. These things we do. In doing them we proclaim ourselves to be members of the Body of Christ.

We begin with what we do "always and everywhere." We want to ask of this doing: Who are we who do these things? What do

13

these things tell us about our Christian identity? We will ask about the basis and goal of our worship in the action of God in Christ. By beginning here with worship—what we take most for granted, indeed what we do almost unconsciously—we will ask about who we are. Here, in the deeds of worship, we act out our response to the one who comes to ask of us, "Adam, where are you?" and "Who do you say that I am?"

B. Liturgy and Life-style

We begin with worship. But what is this worship? Isn't it too hopelessly removed from real life, from important things, to be a very promising starting point? Doesn't this just throw us back into self-preoccupation? What is worship?

The word *liturgy* has a number of connotations for us. Some of us may think with horror of excessively formal and "cold" services of worship. Others may think of the beautiful forms of tradition permeated by the sonorous rhythms of Elizabethan language. But *liturgy* means the work or action of the people of God. Thus whenever we gather together as the people of God we engage in liturgy. Even the most informal gathering for prayer and Bible study is a liturgy. No matter how "restrained" or "enthusiastic," formal or informal, large or small, traditional or avant garde our worship, it is liturgy. It is the common action of the people of God.

We must first notice that we come together to *act*. We do not gather together to be observers of a spectacle, still less to "rest." We come together to act. The New Testament calls the church the *ekklesia*. The *ekklesia* is an assembly. In ancient Greece the citizens were summoned to assemble in order to take action for the defense and welfare of the city as a

14

whole. Only a few of the people were citizens in this sense. Only a few were sufficiently free from working for the necessities of life to take the responsibility appropriate for the whole city. Women, children, slaves, workers, even artisans, were excluded. Only those who were "free" from "having to make a living" were summoned to the assembly. Those immersed in domestic duties, or even in the pursuit of wealth and commerce, did not receive the summons to assemble to take action for the good of the city.[2]

This assembly of the citizens was the *ekklesia*. When the church is called the *ekklesia* it means that it is composed of those who are summoned to take responsibility for the world. But unlike the assembly of the Greeks, this *ekklesia* includes slave and free, male and female, Jew and Gentile, Greek and barbarian. It includes all those who have been set free and summoned to responsibility.

These are those who come together for liturgy—for the work and action of the people of God. When we come together to worship we come together as this assembly of free responsibility in order to act on behalf of the city of God, God's world.

How different our worship looks when seen from this perspective! This is indeed far removed from the concern to be entertained or edified, which we so often make the measure of our worship. We are not slaves of an empire to be entertained with circuses but free citizens gathered to act in concert for the common good.

We are summoned to act. On what basis are we summoned? What is the basis of our action? How do we know what to do? The action of the people of God is a representation and reflection of the action of God in

---

2. See Hannah Arendt's discussion, "The Public and the Private" in *The Human Condition* (Chicago: University of Chicago Press, 1958).

Christ. Our action is not indeterminate or arbitrary. It is a response to the *action of God in Christ*.

This is worth pondering. God has already acted to defend and to save God's own world. This world, which God created and preserved, was nonetheless threatened—with death, with enmity, with sin. Those whom God had created to be the sovereign *lords* of the earth were in fact in bondage, in slavery. Repression and anxiety within, oppression and destruction without are the signs of this bondage. In this situation God has come to us in Jesus to announce deliverance to the captives. And not only to announce but to enact. In the death and resurrection of Christ, the history of the world is transformed from a history of bondage and exile to a history of liberation.

It is in the name of the "Deliverer," this "Liberator," this Christ, that we are summoned to assemble. We have been set free to assume the tasks of freedom. We do not have the task of somehow conjuring up this freedom. We are not the deliverers, the liberators. Rather we are invited and summoned to respond to the word of the Liberator and Deliverer.

The action of the people of God is not an anxious but a glad action. We do not have to begin "from scratch." We are summoned to act out in public that action of God which has already begun to transform the earth. Our action is indeed the public display and acting out of what God has already done and what God will do in Christ. Our action is not arbitrary or indeterminate, not vague or wishful. It is a response to and imitation of the act of God in Christ.

When we speak of worship then we are speaking of an action based on the divine action. But there is more than this in our worship. We must ask about the relationship of this action we

16

perform here to all the other actions of our life in the world.

Too often we think of worship as an escape from the harsh realities of the world, as a respite from our labors, as a sacred time and space separated from the real world. This is a complete misunderstanding. The liturgy we perform should be the model and epitome of our life in the world. In the service of our worship, we model the ways we engage the world in our daily lives.

Paul charges his congregations to present their bodies as a reasonable worship (Rom. 12:1). What does this strange injunction mean? It means that the whole of our life is a true liturgy, an intelligent worship. The body, for Paul, is our way of being in the world. It is in and through our body that we are in relationship to one another and to the structures of life. As bodily beings we have a world. As Kasemann notes, the body is "that part of the world which I am."[3]

To present our bodies then is to present our life in the world, our life in relationship, as an intelligent worship to God. Thus, our true liturgy is our manner of life, our life-style in the world. The liturgy of the gathered community is the epitome, the model, of our life-style, of our way of being in the world.

Liturgy shapes life-style. If we are clear about this then we will have a new perspective on our worship. Far from being a separate "religious activity," our worship is the paradigm for a way of being in the world of politics and economics, the world of responsibility and of labor, the world of relationships.

Dietrich Bonhoeffer called for a nonreligious interpre-

---

3. Ernst Kasemann, "On the Subject of Primitive Christian Apocalyptic," in *New Testament Questions of Today* (Philadelphia: Fortress Press, 1969).

tation of biblical language.[4] By this he meant an interpretation of this language that took seriously its intention to describe our real world and to prescribe a way of being in that world that corresponds to the reality of God in Christ. The great danger Bonhoeffer saw was that Christian faith would withdraw into piety—into separation from the very world Christ had come to redeem. Nowhere is this danger stronger than in our worship, our liturgy. Nowhere does the language we use seem so distant from the world in which we live—the world of international crises, of economic malaise, of political oppression, of social injustice, of environmental catastrophe, of interpersonal pain. But the meaning of Christian faith is that God has come to the real world and draws us into the real world. The real world is where Bonhoeffer lost his life in an attempt to destroy fascism. It is the world where the rich live in comfort while Christ dies on the cross. It is our world. And if, in our worship, we worship in the name of Jesus then we are necessarily engaged in the real world.

We must, therefore, engage in a "nonreligious" interpretation of our liturgy. We must ask how it models a way of being in the world and with our neighbor. We do this not in order to accommodate ourselves to a "secular" or "profane" world but because the Lord we worship is Lord of this world—is its true Liberator.

It is because our liturgy is a response to the action of God in Christ that it has to do with our daily lives in the real world. If we are to understand what we do in the liturgy of the *ekklesia* then we must seek to understand it in relation to our life in the world. We must ask, How does this action serve as a model for a way of actively

---

4. *Letters and Papers from Prison*, ed. E. Bethge (New York: Macmillan Publishing Co., 1953), pp. 195-98, 213-14.

engaging the world in all the days of our lives? Only as it becomes such a paradigm for all of life will our liturgy have a distinctively Christian meaning.

C. The Liturgy of Liberation

In the chapters that follow we will seek to investigate the meaning of one series of actions in our regular worship. We will be trying to understand what we are doing when we confess our sins, when we pray for pardon, when we hear and speak of forgiveness. I will call this sequence of actions the liturgy of liberation. It is the action and work of the people of God, which enacts the liberating activity of Christ.

There are of course a number of other actions we perform in the worship of the congregation, in the liturgy of the *ekklesia*. We offer prayer and we sing praise, we read and expound the word of God, we confess our faith and are sent forth to mission, we drink wine and eat bread. All of these things we do and any of them could be the subject of our reflection.

Of all these actions, however, we will focus on the liturgy of liberation because I believe that this set of actions is the heart and center of our worship. It is here that we say and do those things that represent the inauguration of our life as a life set free from bondage to the law of sin and death. It is here that we display the freedom for which Christ has set us free (Gal. 5:1).

The beginning of the gospel is freedom—deliverance of the captives (Luke 4:18). In the words of confession, repentance, prayer for pardon, and absolution, we enact that freedom. In this work we act out the lierating activity of God. It is indeed a liturgy of liberation.

I know this claim will at first seem odd. We will want to get into something "more   *19* important"—to speak of prayer and praise,[5] or word and sacrament. But none of this can stand without the words of confession and absolution. By focusing here we will gain a perspective on all that we do when we do it together in the name of Christ.

Before we turn directly to the action we perform in the confession and forgiveness of sins it may be helpful to look at the foundation of this action. This will help us to get our bearings and to see what is at stake in this series of actions. We will begin by asking what we mean by the forgiveness of sins. In this we will be helped by considering another part of our worship—the affirmation of faith. Then we will ask about the basis of our action in the action of Jesus. This will make it possible to speak more clearly of the action of the church in the confession and forgiveness of sins.

Then we will be in a position to ask of each of the parts of this action, How does it model a way of being in the world? Thus we will see the confession of sins as a diagnosis of the bondage in which we and the world are imprisoned. We will understand repentance as modeling styles of renunciation that turn us from bondage and its false charms. We will understand the prayer for pardon as a yearning for freedom in which we give voice to the groaning of the whole creation for the liberty of the children of God. We will see the words of absolution as the work of liberation to which we are summoned and so as the meaning of both our responsibility in the *ekklesia* and our life in the world.

In all of this, we will have to attend to both the real basis of our action in the work of God in Christ and the real goal of our action in the liberation of the world.

---

5. The discussion of prayer and praise from the same general perspective will be found in my *Life as Worship: Prayer and Praise in Jesus' Name* (Grand Rapids: Wm. B. Eerdmans Publishing Co., 1982).

"I believe . . . in the forgiveness of sins . . . " 2

I n the creeds of our churches, we confess and affirm that upon which we rely for the meaning of our lives. The creeds are not composed of a series of propositions to which we subscribe, opinions we jointly share. They are not a *set* of beliefs but an *affirmation* of belief. The church in its creed expresses that upon which it relies. If I say "I believe in you," I mean I trust you, I rely on you, I count on you. In the creeds we do not say "I believe that" but "I believe in." The creeds are words the community of faith uses to say upon whom the community finally relies, whom it most fundamentally trusts and depends upon, and to whom it is ultimately loyal.

Thus in the Apostle's Creed we say we rely on God, who creates heaven and earth. We say that we rely on Jesus and say which Jesus we rely on: the one who was born, suffered, died, was raised, and will come. That is, we rely on the Jesus who is known and attested in the New Testament. We rely on this Jesus as the one who founds, shapes, orients, and consummates our lives. We also say that we rely on the Holy Spirit and so on the community of faith and the hope of resurrection. It is in this connection that we say we rely on "the forgiveness of sins."

There is much in this affirmation that many of us find troubling, perplexing, or problematic today. Many of us do not see how these words can represent that upon which we most fundamentally and truly rely for the center, aim, and meaning of our lives. I hope it will be possible for me to deal with some of these questions and perplexities in subsequent essays. For now it will be enough to discuss some of the questions and perplexities occasioned by this one phrase: the forgiveness of sins.

A. Sin and Its Substitutes

What does it mean to believe in, to rely on, the forgiveness of sins? Many of us are uncomfortable with words like *sin, confession, forgiveness.* These words remind us of a pietistic or moralistic past we believe may be best left behind. We know this language has been used to control and manipulate people, to make them "behave." And we know that such language has sometimes had catastrophic consequences causing some to feel themselves incapable of true humanity, to lose hope, to turn inward in self-contempt and despair. Such people assume a crushing burden of guilt and shame, and their lives are crippled by burdens too great to bear. All too often the result is what we today call mental illness. The burden of guilt and of repression exacts its deadly toll in neurosis and even psychosis.

Accordingly we may seek to discover and employ a less destructive language. Instead of sin we may speak of neurosis, mental illness, or "hangups," and instead of forgiveness we may speak of therapy, of self-acceptance, and so on. There are undoubtedly many who have found this "translation" helpful and liberating in moving beyond the careless and destructive use of talk about sin.

Yet this language too has its limitations and its abuses. All too often it encourages a narcissistic self-preoccupation in which a kind of mental health moralism merely takes the place of older forms of moralism. The result is a culture composed of self-preoccupied individuals where healthier-than-thou is a barely disguised substitute for holier-than-thou. It is the culture Christopher Lasch has identified as "the Culture of Narcissism."[1] It is the contemplation of this culture and its effects that has led the psychiatrist Karl Menninger to ask "Whatever became of sin?"[2]

The irony of mental health moralism and therapeutic narcissism is that they leave us finally alone—without community, without the word, which sets us free. We give up talk of salvation only to remain in the same moralizing traps. We have not "thrown out the baby with the bathwater," we have thrown out the baby and kept the bathwater.

One common denominator of both the older (sin) and newer (neurosis) forms of moralism is that they focus on the individual and so encourage us to think almost obsessively of ourselves, to be constantly trying to measure up to some standard of purity or guiltlessness. Perhaps both fail because of their "individualism."

Certainly in our own day we have cause to know that the sin and evil in the world are more fundamental and far-reaching than moralizing talk of sin or neurosis can account for. There are those who therefore wish to leave behind the moralistic and individualistic talk of sin and "self-acceptance" in order to confront the far more pervasive and destructive forces that deform human life in our world. Instead of sin we may speak of

---

1. Christopher Lasch, *The Culture of Narcissism* (New York: W. W. Norton & Co., 1978).
2. Karl Menninger, *Whatever Became of Sin?* (New York: Hawthorn Books, 1975).

oppression, alienation, tyranny, and dehumanization. Instead of forgiveness or therapy we may speak of liberation, justice, and human rights.

Certainly this "translation" is necessary and important. We are indeed so preoccupied with minor questions of morality and mental health that we forget the world and age in which we live is the time and place of the Holocaust. The incineration of the Jewish people appears each day to be but the first installment on horror as we contemplate a nuclear holocaust of which there will be no survivors. Meanwhile most of the nations of the earth live under oppression, the people terrorized by economic exploitation, political tyranny, and the threat of starvation.

If talk of sin causes us to avert our eyes from this reality, then we would surely do better to abandon such talk. After all, Jesus came to proclaim liberty to the oppressed and imprisoned and poor. We will not serve his cause if we turn our backs on these "the least" of his brothers and sisters.

Yet talk of liberation however central to the gospel and urgent for our time may leave important areas of our lives unconsidered. Although we all live in the world of politics and economics we also live in relation to our neighbor, our friend, our spouse, our parents, and our children. There we may find ourselves so trapped and perplexed that we are unable to bear the burden of famine, epidemic, oppression, and exploitation. We may be unable to see that our own perplexities, confusions, and fears have any relation to these "other" issues. If we feel powerless to deal with our own lives how shall we deal with global questions?

The translation of talk of sin into talk of oppression and exploitation may only serve

to increase our sense of powerlessness and

guilt. The more we become aware of how we are racist or sexist, how our comfort is purchased by the misery of millions, how our "security" threatens to destroy the earth, the more we may seek to defend ourselves, to escape from the world's troubles, to become again preoccupied with ourselves.

In this confusion and perplexity we may be aided by the words of our creed. When we say or sing these words we do not say we believe this or that about sin, still less that we believe in sin. We say, "I believe in the *forgiveness* of sins." We rely not on theories (even theological ones) or therapies or political programs, but on the forgiveness of sins. Can this become for us an intelligible and a heartening word? Perhaps it can if we see what this means within the context of the creed itself.

B. The Affirmation of Faith

In order to understand what is at stake in this phrase of our creed it is necessary to see its relationship to other clauses. If we divide the creed into three parts corresponding to the persons of the Trinity then this phrase occurs in the third part introduced by "I believe in the Holy Spirit" following after the affirmation of faith in the Father and the Son. In this formulation of the creed, the church has indicated the universal horizon of God's saving action ("maker of heaven and earth") and has affirmed its faith in the way that saving action has become concrete and definite in Jesus. The faith in Jesus is expressed through reciting events referring to Jesus' past (conceived, born, suffered, crucified, buried, descended), present (sits at the right hand . . .), and future (will come again to judge the living and the dead). This is the context then of what is to follow under the   25 heading of "the Holy Spirit." It is the context of heaven and earth, of past, present, and future.

The Holy Spirit, "the Lord, the giver of life" as the Nicene Creed says, introduces the last five clauses of the creed. Each of these clauses is concerned with life, with our life. The first two clauses designate the immediate realm of our lives: the holy catholic church, the communion of saints. The last two clauses designate the destiny of our lives: "the resurrection of the dead and the life everlasting." Between these two pairs stands the phrase with which we are concerned: "the forgiveness of sins." This placement is not incidental. It provides us with decisive clues for the meaning of our faith.

In the first place the arrangement of the creed suggests a relationship between the forgiveness of sins and the community of faith. It is by virtue of the forgiveness of sins that the church is "holy" and that the community is a "communion of saints." The sanctity and holiness we have ascribed to the universal community of faith is by no means obvious. We know only too well that the church is fragmented, sometimes corrupt, often hypocritical, always fallible and failing. How are we to describe this church as "holy"? Only on the basis of the forgiveness of sins. Apart from this we could never believe in the holy catholic church, or the communion of saints. Moreover, apart from the forgiveness of sins there could be no church. Apart from the message of forgiveness and so of deliverance and redemption, the church could neither have come into being nor continue in being.

Beyond this the forgiveness of sins is the central act of the church's life. In the forgiveness of sins, the church becomes the church—in its message, its worship, its everyday discipleship. That is the point of the church's

26

existence, the goal of its labors, the heart of its life. The church exists in order to participate in the work of forgiving sin. It is for this task that the church is commissioned according to Matthew and John. In the performance of this task, the church is holy—not because it has a corner on virtue but because its action imitates the divine action in the world. The forgiveness of sins then is both the basis and the aim of the church's existence. It is that by and for which the community of faith lives.

The forgiveness of sins is also connected to "the resurrection of the body and the life everlasting." It is the act that prepares for and anticipates the future. In the forgiveness of sins, we are given a future, released from the bondage of the past and from the inexorable fate of becoming past, of passing away. This past of sin and death is overcome in the forgiveness of sins, which anticipates the resurrection of the dead.

Whatever else we may mean by "the resurrection of the body and the life everlasting" we do mean to refer to the promise of God for us and for our world. The promise of God is not that we will transcend our feelings of guilt in order to become a bit more self-affirming, nor is it that by virtue of our work we will be able to make the world a somewhat better place to live in. These are worthy aims to be sure and more will be said about them later, but the promise of God is far more encompassing and radical than these wishes and desires. The reign of God means the abolition of injustice, the reign of peace, the banquet of the Messiah, the abolition of death and sorrow, the coming of the eternal dance and song of joy. These images far exceed all our wildest dreams and fantasies and point to a complete transformation of our lives and world.

This is the transformation indicated by "the resurrection of the body and the life everlasting." And this is the transformation that is already anticipated and enacted in the "forgiveness of sins." No talk of sin however pious, which leads us to forget or to despair of this transformation of heaven and earth, can be that to which our creed refers when it speaks (and we speak) of the forgiveness of sins. The petty moralisms with which talk of sin and its substitutes is so often associated must wither and die in the light of this radical and universal hope.

These final clauses of the creed, in which we also say or sing that we rely on the forgiveness of sins, are introduced by the affirmation of faith in the Holy Spirit. In the Nicene Creed the Holy Spirit is identified as "the Lord, the giver of life." In all that follows we are concerned with life—with our life in community and the abundant life for which we hope. This hope is not in vain for we experience the power of that life here and now in the forgiveness of sins.

It is therefore essential that we understand this forgiveness of sins as a word and deed that gives and demonstrates life. Any understanding of the forgiveness of sins that orients us toward death and guilt, that makes the people of God dis-spirited, cannot be the forgiveness of sins of which the creed speaks.

We know that where the Spirit is, there is freedom (II Cor. 3:17). Accordingly the ways of speaking of sin that result in bondage to guilt, anxiety, and fear cannot be the proper and evangelical understanding, which follows from this creedal formulation, for the Spirit brings freedom and its fruit is joy (Rom. 14:17; Gal. 5:22). The spirited community is the community that enacts this freedom and joy

28

and does so through the forgiveness of sins. We must be sure then that our ways of speaking of sin and its forgiveness point in the direction of this freedom and joy and away from all narrow, legalistic, and mournful self-preoccupation. For what is at stake here is life, abundance and excess of life, life that shatters the bonds of death and overwhelms our guilt with joy.

We began by noticing that talk of sin has become deeply perplexing for many in the community of faith. This talk of sin has too often been associated with petty moralism, narrow legalism, neurotic self-preoccupation, and the desire of some to investigate, control, manipulate, and accuse the lives of others. Moreover it has been used to turn our attention inward and thus away from the reign of sin in the social, political, and economic world.

But by attending to the role that talk of sin plays in the creeds we recite in our common worship, we have come to see that these views of sin are a complete distortion. Christians do not believe *in* sin, do not believe this or that *about* sin. Instead we rely on the *forgiveness* of sins. What we rely on is therefore not a dead and deadly law but a life-giving word and deed. The talk of forgiveness of sins does not leave us alone with our uneasy or easy consciences but places us in community with "the holy catholic church." It does not lead us into dis-spirited preoccupation with guilt but into the freedom and joy that comes from the Holy Spirit. It does not turn us inward upon ourselves but turns us in hope and longing toward the transformation of heaven and earth, the dawning of the reign of God.

We have not yet clarified *how* our talk of sin and of the forgiveness of sins does all these things—that is the task of this book as a whole. But we have at least been able to gain some initial orientation. We know now where we are headed.

Jesus and the Forgiveness of Sins

3

We have seen that talk of the forgiveness of sins places us in relation to the community, to our hope, and to the Spirit. In order to fill out this picture and to substantiate it, it will be helpful to see the role that the forgiveness of sins plays in the New Testament.

A. Jesus Means Freedom

Ernst Kasemann describes the New Testament as the call of freedom. The English translation of his survey of the New Testament as this call to freedom is *Jesus Means Freedom*.[1] A more apt summary of the message of the New Testament can scarcely be imagined. Jesus was called "the Christ." For the Greek this meant the anointed one, but for the Hebrew the anointed one is the one who comes in God's name to deliver God's people. Jesus is the Messiah, the Liberator, and so he is the Christ.

He comes to liberate. He liberates the blind from darkness, the lame from immobility, the sick from disease, the possessed from madness. He shatters the bonds of custom and of class; he breaks open the iron strictures of legalism. He summons the dead to life. He transforms water into wine and death into life. He

---

1. Ernst Kasemann, *Jesus Means Freedom* (Philadelphia: Fortress Press, 1972).

announces deliverance to the captives and sets at liberty those who are oppressed. These are the ways his ministry is described in the Gospels.

This is made especially clear in the Gospel of Luke where Jesus announces his ministry with the words of the prophet Isaiah:

> The Spirit of the Lord is upon me,
> because he has anointed me to preach good news
>   to the poor.
> He has sent me to proclaim release to the captives
> and recovering of sight to the blind,
> to set at liberty those who are oppressed,
> to proclaim the acceptable year of the Lord.
>
> (Luke 4:18-19)

And when the disciples of John come to inquire on their master's behalf whether Jesus is the one for whom they have been waiting, he replies: "Go and tell John what you have seen and heard: the blind receive their sight, the lame walk, lepers are cleansed, and the deaf hear, the dead are raised up, the poor have good news preached to them. And blessed is he who takes no offense at me" (Luke 7:22-23). The whole of the Gospel of Luke is but the narrative elaboration of the truth of Jesus' assertion. By this narrative Jesus is portrayed as the Deliverer and Liberator and thus as the Christ of God.

He is the one who exhibits and enacts sovereign freedom. If, in the beginning, the earthling is commissioned for sovereign freedom as Genesis tells us, then it is in Jesus that we see this sovereignty in act and in word. His contemporaries were amazed, for he spoke (and acted) as one having authority (Matt. 7:29; 21:23).

This freedom, this sovereignty, this au-   *31*

thority is challenged. The world of political and moral and religious law put him to death. Like all those who dare to proclaim freedom and who call others to freedom he earned the enmity of a world in love with its chains. He was crucified. The world's answer to all who are free is death. So it has always been. So it is still.[2]

He claimed freedom and the world gave its answer. He died crying out to the God who had promised freedom to his people: My God, my God, why have you forsaken me? (Mark 15:34).

The early church did not hide this scandal from itself. It knew that the execution of Jesus was either the end or the true beginning of freedom—for all the earth.

The audacious claim of the Christian community is that the death of Jesus is the beginning of life—that his captivity, his disgrace, his execution is the source, the true origin of freedom. It is not the end but the beginning.

The world is turned upside down. The one who is bound, disgraced, and executed in despair is said, by the creeds, to be not only "very man of very man" but also "very God of very God." This broken figure is called the Liberator sent from God, the Christ.

This transvaluation of values is expressed by Paul as "the justification of the ungodly." With this theme Paul works out the understanding of the life, death, and resurrection of Jesus as the liberating activity of God that releases humanity from bondage to the law of sin and death. In Jesus' cross Paul sees the work of liberation and justification brought to a head. It is no longer a question of this or that person being delivered

---

2. For a contemporary illustration of the response of the world to genuine human sovereignty, see my essay "Steve Biko: A Tribute," *Christian Century* 94 (November 2, 1977): 997-99.

from sickness but a matter of the "new creation." It is no longer a matter of this or that person being delivered from the power of demons but of humanity being delivered from the power of death. The work of liberation takes on fundamental depth and universal scope. This is the meaning of the justification of the ungodly.[3]

And when Paul summarizes the effect of this action he speaks of freedom (Gal. 5:1), of the liberty of the children of God (Rom. 8:21). He reserves his sternest rebukes for those who would destroy this freedom (Gal. 5:12). He reminds his readers that they have been freed from bondage, ransomed from slavery, delivered from bondage to the law of sin and death. For Paul, Jesus means freedom and this freedom can be summarized as the justification of the ungodly, as deliverance from sin and death, and so as the forgiveness of sins.

B. The Forgiveness of Sins in the Gospels

The liberating activity of God in Christ has been summarized as the justification of the ungodly and thus as the forgiveness of sin. How does this divine action relate to the action of the community? In order to gain further clarity on this we shall investigate the way in which the forgiveness of sins is presented in the Gospels. We will be asking, How does the action of Jesus determine the action of the disciples?

1. Forgiveness and Healing (Mark)

No Gospel focuses more on the *action* of Jesus than the Gospel of Mark. In this Gospel Jesus is presented as

---

3. The universal scope of justification is the theme of Ernst Kasemann's essay "The Righteousness of God in Paul" in *New Testament Questions of Today*, pp. 168-82.

engaged in an assault on demonic powers represented by sickness of mind and body. His sovereignty is concealed from public view except for this activity of exorcism, an activity that represents the inbreaking of the reign of God.

In the first chapter of Mark, Jesus is introduced, his preaching is summarized (1:15), he is depicted as teaching with authority (1:22), and this authority is demonstrated in an exorcism (1:23-28), the healing of Simon's mother-in-law (1:29-31), a cure of leprosy (1:40-45), and two summary statements: "He healed many who suffered from various diseases, and drove out many devils" and "So all through Galilee he went, preaching in the synagogues and casting out the devils" (1:34, 39 NEB). All of this in the first chapter! What is the meaning of this whirlwind of activity?

In the story of Mark 2:1-12 (the healing of the paralytic), we have an explanation that places us directly before the theme of the forgiveness of sin. When Jesus sees the paralytic (and the faith of those who brought him) he declares, "My son, your sins are forgiven" (2:5 NEB). This is clearly intended by Mark to clarify the meaning of all that has gone before—to bring into focus the character of Jesus' authority. It immediately sparks a controversy among the scribes, to which Jesus responds, "Is it easier to say . . . 'Your sins are forgiven,' or to say, 'Stand up, take your bed, and walk?' " (2:9 NEB). He then commands the paralytic to walk and to the astonishment of onlookers, the man walks!

Several things have happened here that help to clarify the meaning of the forgiveness of sins. Mark makes clear that there is a connection between healing and the forgiveness of sins. What is this connection and how are we to understand it?

34

The power and authority of Jesus to forgive sin is demonstrated by the power of Jesus' word to make the lame walk. Forgiving sin is like healing the sick or overcoming paralysis. It has the effect of setting free, of giving life, of setting in motion. One who had been immobilized by the grip of paralysis is now mobilized by the liberating word: Your sins are forgiven, take up your bed, and walk.

The connection between healing and the forgiveness of sins casts a new light backward over the healings and exorcisms of the first chapter. We see now that Jesus' word is one that liberates his hearers from all that separates them from the wholeness of God's kingdom: from demonic possession, from madness, from weakness, from leprosy, from paralysis, from sin. Indeed sin now means not a moral fault but a binding power, a paralysis, a disfigurement, a being possessed. The word of forgiveness is a liberating word, which overthrows that power, restores health and wholeness, and sets in motion.

Henceforward, when we speak of the forgiveness of sins we must not forget this connection between forgiveness and healing, between sin and bondage. We must keep clear that we are concerned with a liberation that includes the whole person—body, mind, and soul.

That the person is liberated and restored also has a mobilizing effect. The paralytic walks and in walking demonstrates the end of paralysis. Similarly Simon's mother-in-law, who "lay sick with a fever," was set in motion by the healing authority of Jesus. She is last reported serving her guests (1:31). To be liberated, healed, and forgiven is to be set in motion. The importance of this will become clear as we go along.

We should not leave this story without noticing a further feature. When Jesus   35

tells the man that his sins are forgiven, the scribes are
outraged that Jesus has assumed divine prerogatives.
After all it is not a human but a divine right to forgive
sins, and the scribes rightly protest, "It is blasphemy!
Who can forgive sins but God alone?" (2:7). We should
not blame the scribes; they are exactly right, at least
from the standpoint of the Old Testament. Moreover
Mark wants to maintain that Jesus' real identity is
hidden, so we cannot accuse them of not recognizing
that which Jesus conceals. Jesus answers them by first
asking, "Which is easier, to say to the paralytic, 'Your
sins are forgiven,' or to say, 'Rise, take up your pallet
and walk'?" (2:9). Now we are caught. Which do we
really suppose *is* easier? Do we really expect very much
from the forgiveness of sins? Do we not really suppose
that it is little more than a psychological comfort? But to
make a paralyzed man walk—now that's really something! So we might suppose. And we would be dead
wrong! The paralytic walks, but this is the illustration of
that which is far more momentous: His sins are
forgiven. Until we have come to see the forgiveness of
sins as something of astonishing effectiveness that
utterly transforms the situation in which we live and
the forces by which we live, we will have missed the
point.

Jesus demonstrates the authority to forgive sin by the
authority to set a paralytic in motion. He explains
himself by saying, "But that you may know that the Son
of man has authority on earth to forgive sins" (2:10).
Certainly the "Son of man" here refers to Jesus. But is
this all? Is it only Jesus who has this authority? Does
"Son of man" here designate Jesus' peculiar authority?
The story itself makes this quite impossible. The Gospel
of Mark is at great pains to insist that Jesus'
peculiar authority and status is concealed or
hidden until his crucifixion. This is why

36

the demons are commanded to be silent and even those persons who are healed are commanded not to speak of Jesus.

The "Son of man" then must be understood to refer to that humanity which Jesus is announcing and summoning into being. The authority to forgive sins is not an authority restricted to Jesus. It is our authority and responsibility as well. It is this claim of Jesus, a claim he makes not for himself alone but for us as well, that provokes the astonishment and horror of the scribes. The humanity Jesus calls into being is not only a liberated humanity but a liberating humanity.

The dominion of Jesus over demons, over sickness, and over sin is the dominion of "the Son of man"—the earthling created in the image and likeness of God and called into sovereign authority and responsibility over the earth. If this is so then Jesus' authority to forgive sins is an authority we also share. This is certainly the way Matthew understands this same story, for he concludes his version by saying that the crowds "glorified God, who had given such authority to men" (Matt. 9:8, emphasis added).

What we have discovered from this story is an understanding of how forgiveness of sins is a liberating word and deed that overcomes that which separates us from God's reign. As such, the forgiveness of sins is indeed a divine right and action. It is the word and action in which God's rule draws near to us, shattering the bonds we are held by. This divine word and deed however is one that Jesus enacts in the liberation of people from sickness, blindness, madness, and sin. This liberating action finds its center and basis in the forgiveness of sins—to which work we are also summoned.

2. God's Forgiveness and Ours (Matthew)

A connection between God's work of forgiveness and our action is suggested by another series of texts, which are brought to a focus in the petition of the Lord's Prayer: "Forgive us our debts, As we also have forgiven our debtors" (Matt. 6:12). Here we have a direct connection between God's activity of forgiveness and ours. Matthew reports Jesus' stress on this connection: "For if you forgive men their trespasses, your heavenly Father also will forgive you; but if you do not forgive men their trespasses, neither will your Father forgive your trespasses" (Matt. 6:14-15).

So heavily is this point stressed that it is the subject of a parable found only in Matthew's Gospel: the parable of the unmerciful servant (Matt. 18:23-35), who is forgiven but does not forgive and so receives even greater punishment. The parable is concluded with the warning, "So also my heavenly Father will do to every one of you, if you do not forgive your brother from your heart."

Although this connection between our forgiveness and God's is especially characteristic of Matthew it is by no means absent from Luke, who has a parallel petition in the Lord's Prayer (Luke 11:4). Mark, who of course does not have the Lord's Prayer, nevertheless reports another saying with much the same effect: "And whenever you stand praying, forgive, if you have anything against any one; so that your Father also who is in heaven may forgive you your trespasses" (Mark 11:25).

These texts make clear that God's liberating activity is such that it requires of us a response in kind. As God has set us free, so we are commissioned and commanded to set others free. Our action is an imitation of God's action. This is certainly not to be regarded as something optional. It is indeed made the condition of God's forgiveness—namely, that we forgive. Beyond that the community of Jesus actually prays, Forgive as we forgive! We ask God to deal with us as we deal with our neighbors—to liberate us as we liberate them! We actually do this regularly—every time we recite the Lord's Prayer in public or private. We do it absentmindedly—yet it is the most audacious and terrifying moment in our worship. We who hold grudges, charge interest, exclude sinners, ignore oppression; we ask God to deal with us as we deal with our neighbors!

There is another side to this connection between God's forgiveness and ours. It is that God's forgiveness is such that it is continued in the world by our forgiveness of our neighbor. The divine action has a kind of ripple effect. To be forgiven is to become forgiving; to be liberated is to engage in liberation. Our action is launched by God's action and is a continuation of and witness to that action. When we forgive another, when we release another, when we heal another, we demonstrate the work of God in the world, who comes to free people.

Matthew's parable of the great judgment (25:31-46) makes this abundantly clear, for it makes our action of mercy and liberation the determining factor in our relation to God. Our deeds of concrete assistance to "the least of these" determine whether or not we enter the "kingdom prepared for you from the foundation of the world."

These texts then bring us closer to an understanding of the importance and character of what we do when we come together to confess our sin and hear and announce the forgiveness of sin. When we do this we respond to the liberating activity of God in Christ. That liberating activity is given effect in and through our action.

We have gained a partial answer to the question of our authority and responsibility to forgive and so to be participants in the "liturgy of liberation." Thus far we have seen that we forgive those who have offended us as a demonstration of God's having forgiven us for having offended God. But what of the way our neighbor is separated from God? Do we have power and authority there as well?

3. *The Commission (John)*

To answer this question we turn to another set of texts in which Jesus authorizes his disciples to act directly on God's behalf in the forgiving of sins. Matthew reports this commission twice, once in response to Peter's confession of faith (Matt. 16:19) and then again as part of a general teaching directed to *all* his disciples: "Whatever you bind on earth shall be bound in heaven, and whatever you loose on earth shall be loosed in heaven" (Matt. 18:18). The second commission is found in a whole series of sayings concerning forgiveness of sins, so there can be no doubt that Matthew thought of the commission to bind and loose in connection with the forgiveness of sins. Here a precise parallel is drawn between the action of the disciple and the action of God. That which we forgive, loose, or absolve on earth is also forgiven and absolved in heaven. Now it is made explicit that we are the agents of the divine forgiveness—that we are commissioned to forgive in God's name—that through our activity of forgiving, God also forgives.

We are in this respect charged with no less an authority than that which Jesus claims for the Son of man—to perform the deed of God. Like Jesus we are commissioned to release people from the paralysis and bondage of sin—from all

40

that separates them from the reign of God. We are made full participants in the work of liberation, which anticipates the kingdom of God.

The point is underscored in the commission Jesus gave to his disciples in John's Gospel. The author of this Gospel was at some pains to make clear that the Spirit of God, the direct divine empowerment, is not given to the disciples until Jesus' resurrection. It is the risen Lord then who addresses his disciples, "As the Father sent me, so I send you." He then breathed on them saying, "Receive the Holy Spirit! If you forgive any man's sins, they stand forgiven; if you pronounce them unforgiven, unforgiven they remain" (John 20:21-23 NEB).

Several points call for remark in connection with this passage. First, there is a direct parallel between the authority of Jesus and the authority of the disciple: "As the Father sent me, so I send you." This culminates a whole series of parallel assertions concerning the disciple and Jesus including the assertion of Jesus in John 17:21 that just as the Son and Father are one so also are the disciples one with the Son. Rather than attempting to collect all the illustrations of this parallel let us content ourselves with the recognition that it exists. Even if this text stood alone it would be breathtaking. It confers upon the one who receives Jesus' word an authority that is a direct reflection of the sovereignty of God. Jesus summons us to an astonishing dominion and authority.

These words anticipate the next point. Jesus breathes the Spirit on his disciples. This is John's version of the Pentecost story of Acts 2. But it is told now against the background of Genesis 2:7. Those who in their creation receive the breath of life, now in their re-creation receive the breathing   *41* of the Holy Spirit.[4] We are mobilized into life. This is how we are sent. We are re-created by being sent. To be is to be commissioned.[5]

And this commission is summarized as one of authority over sin: What you forgive is forgiven. As the earthling was created in the image and likeness of God and given dominion over the earth, so now the disciples of Jesus are re-created in the likeness of his commission and given authority over sin—over that which separates God's world from God's reign. We are commissioned to be the agents and representatives of the divine sovereignty. This and nothing less is the meaning of the liturgy of liberation we enact in our worship in the confession and forgiveness of sin.

4. Judgment

In the commission to exercise authority over sin and so over that which separates us, our neighbors, and our world from God, we are the representatives of God's own liberating activity. We are called to represent God. But which God? We are called to bind and loose in God's name, but what is to be bound, what loosed? Are

---

4. Both at the beginning (John 1:1-14) and at the end (John 20:21-23) of John's Gospel we are referred back to the opening verses of Genesis in such a way as to be led to understand that Jesus is the new beginning, the new creation.

5. The poem of Genesis 1:1–2:4a, which is in the background of John's Gospel, is organized as a series of commissions. The "firmament" is commissioned to "separate the waters" (1:6); the earth is commissioned to "put forth vegetation" (1:11); the sun and moon are commissioned to "rule over the day and over the night" (1:18). The culmination of this series comes with the appearance of the earthling as male and female, commissioned to be the image and likeness of God (1:26-28). This divine commission to represent God on earth is specified here in the Gospel of John as the commission to forgive sins.

these actions equal in importance and in ultimacy?

There is no way to answer this question abstractly. We must answer it by asking what God we are to represent in our binding and loosing. The texts we have considered already prepare the answer to this question. The God whose action we represent is the one who comes to loose, to liberate, to save. God does not cause paralysis, leprosy, madness. Rather God liberates from these conditions. Our action must be similarly unambiguous. We are to bring not paralysis but freedom. The God whose action we are to imitate does not arbitrarily judge here and save there but judges in order to save, binds demons in order to save people. God's no does not stand alongside God's yes. The no is wholly subordinate to the yes.[6] It is no less severe for all of that. It is no less judgment for being subordinated to salvation, but it is subordinate.

The "binding" in which we engage should certainly not be an arbitrary deed. It must only take place after long and careful reflection and mutual interrogation and admonition. The picture we have from the early church is as follows. After long and patient discussion with a person, the community as a whole may decide that his or her manner of life fundamentally opposes the divine love and overthrows the liberty and love that is supposed to characterize the life of the community. Accordingly the person is bound over to Satan (I Cor. 5:5). This means that the community publicly disavows this action or style of life. This should only be done in extreme

---

6. This is the interpretation of "double predestination," which we find in Karl Barth's Church Dogmatics II, 2 (Edinburgh: T. & T. Clark, 1957), pp. 306-506. This revision of the doctrine of election is the single most important contribution of Barth's theology to the church's self-understanding.

circumstances where the integrity of faith and life is at stake. The aim of the action is to clarify the witness of the community of faith to the crucified and risen Lord.

Yet there can be no doubt that this witness is best clarified through the forgiveness of sins. That is precisely the aim Paul sets for the drastic step of delivering a sinner to satan in I Corinthians 5:5. Indeed, we know only too well that hastily and arbitrarily condemning diverse styles of life and diverse formulations of faith becomes not a sign of the divine grace and liberation but the countersign of human arrogance and pettiness. All too often the desire to clarify or purify the life and witness of the community of faith abolishes the love of God made manifest in the cross. For this reason the church wisely rejected the rigorist policies of the Montanists and the Donatists in the early centuries of its life.

There could really be no possibility of misunderstanding this. Have we not heard that we will be forgiven as we have forgiven? Do we need to be reminded that our binding and retaining subjects us to judgment? It is in this connection that we may recall the often repeated injunction, "Judge not" (Matt. 7:1-3; Luke 6:37-38; Rom. 14:1-13).

But we are authorized to bind as well as loose, to retain as well as forgive. That is undoubtedly true. We must undoubtedly oppose all that which binds and breaks people. In this opposition to the paralyzing and disfiguring power of sin and death, we must bind the "strong man" in order to release his captives. We cannot be patient with sin, with oppression, with disease, with all that destroys God's children. But toward God's people themselves we must be the agents of liberation, of the divine deliverance and mercy.

In the Genesis account of the creation and ordination of the earthling as the image and

44

likeness of God, we are told that the earthling is to have dominion over the earth. It is remarkable in this account that no dominion is given over the earthling, over the other person. Here too, in the work of forgiveness, we are given no authority over our neighbor. We cannot judge the neighbor. But we can and must liberate the neighbor, and in doing so we will bind sin in order to deliver the neighbor. Our authority is real but it is limited.

And so it is as well with God in Christ, who comes to us to deliver us from condemnation. In the imagery of the New Testament, it is said that he does this by taking our condemnation upon himself. He binds himself in order to loose us.[7]

And if it is so for him is it different for us? The Gospel of Mark from which we began this exploration of the meaning of forgiveness repeatedly admonishes the disciples to follow the way of Jesus. They who are commissioned with authority over sickness and demons (over that which separates us from God) are shown the way that authority must be exercised: Take up your cross and follow me (Mark 8:34; cf. Mark 9:35, 10:43-45).

This is the character of our authority and sovereignty over sin: that we participate in the death of him whose death is our life, whose condemnation is our liberation. When we take up the liturgy of liberation we take up this work and this way.

Conclusion

The way the New Testament speaks of the forgiveness of sins validates and clarifies the way in which the creed speaks of the same subject. In the ministry of Jesus as displayed by Mark's Gospel, we see the forgiveness of sins as the act that inaugurates and demon-

---

7. Ibid.

strates the reign of God. Thus the overthrow of the power of death in healing and exorcism is given its basis in the forgiveness of sins.

In John's Gospel the commission and authorization to forgive sins is made the meaning and demonstration of the presence and power of the Holy Spirit. To receive the Spirit, to be spirited, is to receive this commission and authority.

But most important, not only in Mark and John but throughout the New Testament, we find that the work of the forgiveness of sins is *our* work. It is the life for which we are commissioned and empowered. Insofar as we engage in this healing and liberating activity, we demonstrate the power and love of God, which transforms all things and justifies the ungodly.

When we say that we rely on the forgiveness of sins, we first assert that we rely on the one who forgives, heals, and liberates us. But beyond this we mean that we rely on this commission to participate in God's own mission and ministry to and in the world. Our action follows from God's action; it is the continuation and representation of God's action. This means that we rely on God to act in and through our action—to make of our words and deeds what they can never be by themselves—the sign and seal of God's own liberating and saving action.

That we rely on God's action means that we emulate that action—that we engage in the work of the forgiveness of sins. But how are we to do this? How can our action be brought into conformity and continuity with God's act? Together as the gathered community of faith we act out the pattern for our life as the liberated and liberating community. It is to this action of the church, of the assembly of the free, that we must turn if we are to understand how our life may have this character.

46

The Liturgy 4

We turn now to consider directly the liturgy of liberation. In this liturgical sequence of confession, repentance, prayer for pardon, assurance, and forgiveness, the weighty theological theme of justification is expressed concretely and corporately in the life of the gathered community. Here we enact the meaning of the liberating action of God in Christ. This enactment has become so familiar to us that we may have forgotten how much is at stake in it—how directly it expresses the liberty of the children of God. Attention to this liturgical sequence may help us to recover a sense of the meaning of our Christian identity in the world.

In this chapter, I will first say something of the history and place of this liturgy of confession, repentance, and absolution.[1] This brief sketch will help reveal the importance of this action in the life of the Christian community. I will then briefly describe something of the character and meaning of each of the elements of this action, beginning with the aim or goal of the action and then working backward through the sequence: absolution, words of assurance, prayer for pardon, repentance, confession, and call to confession.

---

1. A detailed study of the development of the practice of penance may be found in Karl Rahner's *Theological Investigations, Vol. XV: Penance in the Early Church* (New York: Crossroads Publishing Co., 1982).

47

In this way we will be able to see how each of these acts is integrated into a single action on the basis of the goal of the action as a whole. This will prepare the way to discuss more extensively in the chapters that follow all of these actions as models and epitomes of the Christian life.

A. Sin After Baptism

Before the actions of confession and absolution could take their place in the worship of the community, it was necessary to deal with the question of sin after baptism. To many in the early church, it seemed simply unthinkable that people who had confessed their faith in Jesus and had been baptized in his name should fail thenceforward to live blameless lives. There was, after all, Christ's command to be perfect "as your Father in heaven is perfect" (Matt. 5:48 GNB). Similarly, John maintained: "No one born of God commits sin" (I John 3:9), and the letter to the Hebrews warned that "it is impossible to restore again to repentance those who have once been enlightened" (Heb. 6:4). The problem was especially acute in the era of persecution. If Christians renounced their faith for fear of persecution or death then surely they had forfeited their right to belong to the community or to take part in its worship. But by extension any sin was in greater or lesser degree also apostasy, a renunciation of the sacrifice of Christ, a yielding to the principalities and powers of the old world. Accordingly many communities insisted on excluding from their ranks all those who fell into sin.[2]

---

2. This rigorism was the policy of the second-century prophet Montanus. Tertullian, the first Latin theologian, held a similar view and so was regarded as "tainted" with the heresies of Montanus. In subsequent centuries the Donatists carried on this rigorism until decisively defeated by Ambrose and Augustine.

These had shown who was their true lord, to whom they owed true allegiance. To take them in again would only bring the community and its Lord into disrepute. Thus the community should "deliver [them] to Satan" (I Cor. 5:5).

The counter-argument was quickly launched. It was launched not in the name of moral laxity but in the name of the gospel. The church was commissioned both to bind and to loose. If it renounced the right to absolve it also renounced the right to bind.[3] Even more important however was the clear and repeated injunction against judging our neighbor (Matt. 7:1-3; Luke 6:37-38). If we exclude the neighbor from our fellowship and from the grace of Christ mediated through the sacrament then we violate the command of Christ. Not the sinner but the church would then be guilty of apostasy. In the name of Christ, we would instead be proclaiming an anti-Christ.

The debate, clearly, was not about rigorous versus lax standards of discipline. It was about the identity of Christ and his community. In this debate the rigorist party lost. It lost not because people favored laxity but because they were persuaded that obedience to Christ required the forgiveness of sins. After all Christ came to the lost and none of them would be members of his body save for the divine mercy. To favor the forgiveness of sins was not to take sin lightly but to take grace more seriously. Of course there is a great risk here as the rigorists had seen, for to take grace seriously means that we risk forgetting both the power and the gravity of sin. It means that we may turn baptism into a mere ceremony and the Christian life into a cultural convention. It means that we may find ourselves in the situation of being unable to

---

3. Ambrose, *Two Books Concerning Penance* (ca. 384), Book I, ch. 2, no. 7.

reply when asked what difference being a Christian really makes. What begins by taking grace seriously may end by making grace cheap.

As I have said, the church decided against the rigorist policy. But it could not ignore the importance of the objections to too easy an accommodation to human weakness and sin. The rejection of rigorism made the liturgy of confession and repentance *possible*. The obvious dangers of cheap grace made the liturgy *necessary*. It quickly assumed a place of great importance in the life of the church. It took its place alongside baptism and the Lord's Supper as a sacrament—a place it held universally until the Reformation. Even with the Reformation it very nearly kept that place. Luther at first argued for its sacramental character even though he rejected the medieval view that confirmation, ordination, marriage, and extreme unction were sacraments.[4] Only after much deliberation did he finally exclude penance and then he did so while maintaining that though it was not a sacrament it was nonetheless crucial for the life of faith and could not be neglected. It has, in the meantime, fallen into neglect in the churches of the Reformation. This neglect has once again threatened to turn the Christian church into contending parties: on the one side those for whom Christian identity is merely a phrase licensing every form of cultural accommodation; and on the other, those who seek to reclaim Christian identity by reimposing moralistic and legalistic structures of belief and practice. This is the situation in which we find ourselves. This is the situation in which it becomes important, indeed urgent, to ask, What is the meaning of the forgiveness of sins?

---

4. Martin Luther, "The Sacrament of Penance" (1519), *Luther's Works*, v. 34.

B. Private Confession and Public Liturgy

In the history of the church, the ritual of forgiveness has had a double character. At first the confession and repentance of sin after baptism was a public act performed by the penitent. This act, together with the absolution pronounced by the priest on the community's behalf, restored the sinner to the community and its worship.

Subsequently this practice was abandoned in favor of a dual practice. On the one hand the restoration of the individual sinner to the community took place in the private confessional with the priest. This became the locus of the sacrament of penance. On the other hand the worship of the community included the practice of a general confession and repentance for the community as a whole.

The sacrament of penance (repentance) was accordingly associated in the (Western) church with the private confession to the priest. This became the basic form of "pastoral care" in the life of the community. It was here that the conscience of the Christian was examined and here that the individual Christian was assigned the work of satisfaction, which would restore him or her to the fellowship of the community. So indispensable did this practice become that it was made a condition for admission to the sacrament of the mass or eucharist. Thus the confession and repentance of sin came to be understood not as the extraordinary act of the exceptional sinner—but as the appropriate activity of all Christians.

Two consequences follow from this change in perception and practice. First, the community acknowledges the pervasiveness of sin in its members. It exhibits an awareness that   *51* bondage and brokenness are a continuing feature of our life against which we are continually having to do battle. But second, the tendency grows toward a kind of moralism that understands sin less as bondage and brokenness than as specific actions to be avoided or for which precise penalties could be paid. With this latter development, the doors were opened to the abuses of the penitential system against which the Reformation protested.

The challenge then is to build an understanding of this practice and action that avoids the abuses to which it was subjected while still providing for its initial recognitions:

(a) that grace abounds more than sin
(b) that sin is still to be taken seriously
(c) that Christian existence continually struggles against the forms of bondage and brokenness from which Christ came to liberate humanity.

C. The Liturgy

In this reflection we will attend to the public and general forms of this liturgy. It is from the practice that is universal in the church rather than from the special features of the sacrament of penance as it is still practiced in part of the church that we must seek to understand this action and practice.

Concerning the practice of confession-repentance-absolution in our general worship we may begin by noticing two features: that it is a corporate action and that it is a regularly repeated practice.

Above all here we are concerned with a public and corporate practice. As a liturgical form it has remained relatively unchanged through the history of the community. But we focus on it

52

not only because this is the common form of the practice. Our concern here is with Christian identity as that is displayed in our coming together, in our assembling for action as the *ekklesia*. It will be crucial therefore to keep clearly in view that when we confess our sin, repent and pray for pardon, and hear or pronounce words of absolution, we do this not as isolated individuals but as members of a community. Neither in sin nor in its renunciation nor in its absolution do we stand alone.

It is not only a corporate action, it is also a repeated one. Whenever we come together to worship we confess, repent, hear, and speak absolution. The community that acts in this way is not a community of the perfected but of the struggling. The *ekklesia* is not the church victorious but the church militant, always in need of confession, repentance, and forgiveness. By participating in this liturgy we enact the once-and-for-all action of God in Christ. But *we* do not enact it once and for all, we enact it again and again. Our action is thus differentiated from that action to which it points. It is nevertheless a continuation and perpetuation of that unique action.

That we repeat this action means that it is an abiding form of our life together and in the world. It is not something we finish in order to go on to something else. It is the constantly renewed beginning of all of our life.

In our services of worship, we find some or all of the actions of the following sequence: call to confession, confession of sins, repentance, prayer for pardon, words of assurance, pronouncement of absolution. What is the meaning of this sequence and how is it to be understood?

We begin with the observation that the meaning of any sequence is likely to be found 53

in its climax or consummation, in the final action. The end is the point or aim that expresses the meaning of all other actions in the sequence that lead up to it. Accordingly, now, in the last half of this chapter, I will describe and interpret this sequence from the end to the beginning. This will prepare us to consider the meaning of each of the elements of the sequence.

1. Absolution

The meaning of our actions in this sequence is contained in the words: I absolve you—I release you—I forgive you. These words are the culmination of the series of actions with which we are concerned. What is the meaning of this action?

We should first note that this is the one action in this sequence which is the subject of Christ's commission to forgive, to bind, and to loose. It is therefore the crucial moment in this liturgy. All else elaborates or develops this point. All else prepares for this act and work.

Absolution means *release*. In the words of absolution, the speaker releases the hearer from a kind of bondage. The words of absolution are the words of liberation. In this we may be reminded of Jesus and the paralytic. To forgive is to release from paralysis, from immobility, from bondage and imprisonment. It is this toward which our action points.

Absolution is the word of *authority*. Often in our liturgies this which is the aim or point of the action is omitted. We do this, it is often said, because only God can pronounce absolution—only God can set free. There is considerable truth in the principle—and considerable falsehood in the practice. It is of course true that that which has been accomplished in Christ is both unrepeatable and unsurpassable. In his life, death, and resurrection we are summoned from death to life, and the power of bondage and brokenness is dealt the decisive blow. But it is nevertheless true that we are summoned to imitate and so continue that action through forgiving our neighbor and so through loosing and binding of sin. To evade this task in our worship or in our life is to evade the clear command of the one we call Lord.

Absolution, release, and forgiveness must then be announced and enacted if our liturgy is to be an action that imitates and corresponds to the action and word of Christ. But this means that we publicly and corporately enact the sovereign authority to which we are called. There is no way to minimize the scandal of this authority. In God's stead and in God's name we pronounce the forgiveness of sins. We exorcize the demons, and we command the dissolution of the bonds of disfigurement and paralysis, which separate our neighbor from God.

This is the moment toward which this whole sequence points. We do not begin properly unless we begin toward *this* end, aim, conclusion. It is of no use whatever to recognize or to repent of sin if the recognition and repentance are not a movement toward this end. The only sin we know, says Karl Barth, is sin that has already been forgiven. We do not really see the problem until we have been grasped by the solution. We cannot hear the question until we have been confronted with the answer. We do not know the depth of our captivity until we are released. The "revolution of rising expectations" holds true here as well as for the movements of social and political change. We do not oppose our chains unless we have hope for freedom.

Absolution, which stands at the end of this sequence, is therefore its true beginning.

55

2. Words of Assurance

We pronounce absolution, we forgive sin. We really do this; but we do not do it alone. We do not manufacture our own authority. In acting as we do here we do not act rashly but confidently. We act not as a wager, a venture, a gamble, but with assurance.

We are not left in doubt concerning the desire and promise of God. We know that if we confess our sins God will forgive them. We know that no power either in the world or in our hearts can finally separate us from God's love (Rom. 8:38-39). We know God's promise and know that it can be relied on. We do not, therefore, act either rashly or timidly here. We act on the basis of God's action and promise.

Beyond this we act as we are commanded to act. There is here nothing of a voluntarism. We, the community of Christ, are commissioned and authorized to announce this forgiveness, to demonstrate and perform it. The "power of the keys" is entrusted to us as a demonstration of God's freedom to liberate. Those whom God liberates God makes participants in liberating action. As Paul says, God gives us not the spirit of slavery but of freedom (Rom. 8:15-21). We proclaim and enact this freedom and responsibility when we pronounce and perform absolution.

The reciting of "words of assurance" therefore points to the ground of our action in God's action. These words remind the community of the way its authority is authorized, of the way in which its sovereignty is commanded and commissioned, of the way its freedom derives from and corresponds to the liberating action of God in Christ.

The words also assure the hearer of

absolution that the forgiveness here administered is not partial, fragmentary, arbitrary, or mistaken forgiveness. When a member of the community declares "I absolve you" she or he speaks in the name and with the authorization of God. The words of assurance therefore exclude the possibility that our anxiety will drive a wedge between the action and word made visible here and the action and word of God. The words of assurance summon faith to confidence and so to deliverance from all anxiety and fear.

3. Prayer for Pardon

How are we to be situated in order to hear this comforting, strengthening, and liberating word? In the prayer for pardon, we turn toward this liberating word in yearning and expectation. The prayer for pardon is a prayer. It is accordingly a turning toward God, toward God's promise. It is a claiming of that promise for ourselves.

Once again, the promise of God is not uncertain. God has promised the kingdom, the reign, the coming to us in mercy and with deliverance. The life, death, and resurrection of Christ has clarified and ratified this promise. In Christ's life and death we learn that the reign of God means healing of mind and body, means the overthrow of injustice and oppression; the abolition of anxiety, and fear, and sorrow; the vanquishing of sin and death. When we pray we turn ourselves toward this promised deliverance and liberation. We pray for pardon and so for the coming of the one who conquers all that separates God's world from God's reign.

In this prayer for pardon, we turn in yearning and in expectation to the one who saves and liberates. We declare ourselves to be those who live in hope
and whose lives are turned toward the future,
toward freedom, toward God.   57

4. Repentance

We turn toward the future and toward freedom. But this turning toward means as well a turning away. It means a turning away from our bondage, a renunciation of our paralysis, a refusal of that which seduces us from freedom and solicits our collaboration in our own bondage and brokenness.

We cannot turn toward freedom without turning against bondage. We cannot turn our face toward God's promise without turning our back on that which opposes that promise. The more confidently we turn toward freedom the more resolutely we turn against the captivity of the past. Hence the words: "We do earnestly repent." We do seriously and heartily turn away from all the ways we have identified ourselves with our bondage, from all the ways we have permitted ourselves to be lured away from freedom.

Repentance is not to be understood moralistically or legalistically therefore. It is an act of freedom. It is a protest against and renunciation of bondage. It is not important for its own sake but for the sake of turning toward freedom. It is not done to placate a wrathful lawgiver but to turn toward the merciful Deliverer. It is therefore not done to earn favor. It is a response to the promise and the fact of liberation.

Great harm is done if we fail to keep clear the proper relation between repentance and absolution. For when repentance is severed from the absolution that is its true goal it becomes an anxious work and an all-the-more-severe captivity of the conscience. In repentance we turn away from bondage because we are turning toward freedom; that freedom which is already 58 promised to us by the action of God in Christ.

5. Confession

We turn away from bondage. But which bondage? If our action is to be clear and certain we must see and acknowledge the specific and concrete forms of bondage in which we find ourselves. We must do this in such a way that we actually recognize in the words of our confession our real situation and need. Accordingly we confess our sins.

Here is a point of sober and clear-sighted self-assessment. For here we declare not who we would like ourselves to be but who we really are. We acknowledge our bondage and brokenness. If we are oblivious to this we cannot turn away from it or toward the promised freedom.

Yet this disclosure and recognition does not stand alone or by itself. We are not engaged in a process of self-exposure for its own sake. We see this bondage and brokenness only in the light of the liberation that is promised and made manifest in Christ. Indeed the more clearly we see the dimensions and radicality of the promised liberation, the more acutely we will be aware of the chains we clutch to ourselves. It is only because we genuinely hope for freedom that we see the dimension and depth of our bondage. This is why so many of the greatest exemplars of faith have accused themselves of the greatest sin. The stronger our hope the greater our impatience with the vestiges of death and bondage that still ensnare us.

This recognition of sin in the light of hope is a far cry from despairing self-preoccupation, which is the characteristic of a confession of sin that has lost its connection to the assurance of absolution. The point of a confession of sin is not to dwell in the swamp of self-accusation, self-contempt, self-preoccupation. It is rather to leave all this behind, to renounce it, and to turn in yearning and confident expectation of the freedom promised. This is why it is so crucial that confession occur within this sequence governed by absolution. We see our sin, our bondage and brokenness, in the light of forgiveness.

6. *The Call to Confession*

We are therefore summoned and summon one another to enter into this awareness, this disclosure, this recognition; not in order to despise ourselves but because God has come to us and will come to us in mercy, love, and power to deliver and liberate us. In the call to confession, we announce the end of our action at the beginning. We indicate the basis and goal of the action in advance: "Let us confess our sins *knowing* that God will forgive."

Conclusion

We engage together in this sequence of actions when we come together to perform the liturgy of the *ekklesia*. In the repetition of this action, we become practiced in these actions—in the recognition of our situation, in the renunciation of bondage, in the turning toward freedom, in the pronouncement and performance of liberation. How does this shape our lives in the world? This is the question we must explore in the chapters that follow.

PART TWO

Interpretations

Confession

5

I n our common worship we are summoned and invited to "confess our sins." This is not the only "confession" we perform in our worship. We also join in the confession of our faith. We have already seen that in this second confession or affirmation we say that we rely on the forgiveness of sins. That we do in fact rely on this is evident from our participation in the first, the confession of our sins.

A. The Diagnosis of Bondage

When we confess our sins we do not engage in an act of shame-faced self-abnegation. We act with the freedom and confidence of the children of God. In our confession of faith, we identify ourselves as those who rely on God's act and promise. In the confession of our sins, we identify ourselves as those who need and desire this divine act and promise.

We confess our need and identify ourselves with this need. This is true of all our prayer. In prayer we express our need for God. This goes to the very heart and core of our being. The Old Testament speaks of the earthling as a *nephesh*.[1] We translate this as "soul" and by this mean the very center of our being. But what is this center?

---

1. For an extended discussion of *nephesh*, see Hans Walter Wolff, *Anthropology of the Old Testament* (Philadelphia: Fortress Press, 1974), pp. 10-25.

Nephesh means first of all the throat. The Old Testament uses this as a metaphor for all the ways in which our existence is an existence of need and lack: the need for air, for food, for water. By extension this also means our need for companionship, for justice, for help, for God. To be a *nephesh* is to be in need. This is who we are. Our prayer is an expression of our soul; our need, lack, and yearning.

When we confess our sin we identify our need and lack to the one who comes to us to meet this need. But here it is not just any need or lack we express. It is our sin. Our need is not simply the need of the creature dependent on God for life and well-being but the need of the broken creature for liberation and forgiveness. We do not confess our creatureliness but our sin. We acknowledge that we are separated from the one whom we need in order to live.

The confession of sin is then a confession of our bondage and brokenness, of the distortion and disfigurement of our creatureliness. We are not only creatures but fallen creatures. We not only need God but are actually without God and against God. In the confession of sin, then, we see ourselves in the light of the divine liberation, in the light of the justification of the ungodly. It is in this light we see that we are actually in bondage, that we are truly the "ungodly." We see ourselves as those in need of liberation.

Thus the confession of sin is not concerned primarily with moral faults or habitual failings. It is concerned with our fundamental condition before God. This condition is not reducible to moral shortcomings. Paul calls it bondage to the law of sin and death (I Cor. 15:56; Rom. 8:2) and the Gospel of Mark likens it to paralysis, madness, and 63 leprosy. The Gospel of John likens it to darkness and death. It is a radical and complete distortion of our being.

Our life is not described in this way because of a misanthropic cynicism. It is described in this way because of the kind of liberation we hope for on the basis of the promise and action of God in Christ. We see our condition in the light of the Resurrection, as bound to the law of sin and death. We can "moderate" our talk of sin only by "moderating" our talk of redemption. To suppose that we are essentially in pretty good shape is to refuse to hope for anything much different. Awareness of sin is a counsel of hope rather than despair. If we are offended by talk of sin it is because we have ceased to hope for the transformation God promises.

To confess our sin then is to be acutely aware of our separation from God, from the God who comes to us, and from the God who comes to us in no other way than the cross. In the confession of sin, we see our bondage and brokenness as radical and complete because we see it in the light of God's radical and complete liberation.

But if we were to leave the matter here we would be in danger of rendering terms like *sin* and *grace* quite abstract and general. The liberation to which our actions here must correspond is one that engages our life in its concrete relations and situations. Thus we are concerned with the specific forms of our bondage and brokenness when we confess our sin.

Sin comes to expression in *sins*. Sins are the symptoms of sin. Our fallenness is not only a basic distortion of our being—it is also expressed in and through particular forms of bondage and brokenness in our daily lives. We are thus concerned here with the way original sin becomes actual sin, with the way a fundamental distortion has particular manifestations. We confess not only our sin but our sins.

Confession of sins must not become a random recitation of imagined faults but instead must be a sober assessment of our condition. We do not need to be at a loss here about what is appropriate to confess. Quite simply we are concerned with the particular ways we resist the freedom for which Christ has set us free.

We confess then the ways in which we remain bound and paralyzed by an anxiety that prefers itself to faith. We confess the ways in which we are continually at war with the summons to freedom, the ways we are bound up by resentment, envy, and enmity. We confess the ways we collaborate in the structures of oppression and deprivation, which keep God's children from the freedom, justice, and bounty God has intended for them. These are the things that must be exposed here, for these are the ways we resist and oppose the divine liberation.

They are as well the ways in which we are bound. We fear rejection and so are not free to love. We fear we will be abandoned, so we seek to control and possess those who love us—killing their love or making it worthless. In our fear of being abandoned, we make ourselves alone. We fear that people will shun us if they know the truth about us, so we hide behind masks and are more alone than if we had been shunned. We paralyze ourselves with fear and anxiety and secret dread. We put ourselves under lock and key.

We think love is a scarce good so we give ourselves over to jealousy—and know neither love nor peace. We think our neighbor's advantage must be our disadvantage, so we grumble about the poor, the black, the women, the young. We seek to put them under lock and key: their place, their station in life, their proper role. Repression within, oppression without. We are slaves of our fear, our resentment, our anxiety.

We even do this with our religion. We hide from God behind our morality, behind our religiousness. We flee from God by becoming pious. We use the language of faith to conceal our unbelief. We use the name of Jesus to worship an idol of our own imaginings. We want God to be a tribal deity—protecting us from "them": protecting our values, our way of life, our privileges. We make God the emblem of our anxiety and fear and resentment.

These are the things needing to be expressed in our confession. These are the things that destroy us.

We express these things clearly and incisively not in order to "wallow" in our guilt but because these are the specific forms of bondage from which we need and want and expect to be liberated. We need to be quite clear here about the identity of the God to whom we direct this confession. Is this the god of a deified superego who pitilessly accuses us? Is this the god who is an implacable law, exacting of us a scrupulous legalism? Is this a god who is a cosmic busybody concerned with sniffing out our every minor flaw? Or do we confess to the One who comes to us to liberate us and to bring us into the kingdom of love and liberty? who enters deeply into our condition—even to death on the cross, becoming sin who knew no sin (II Cor. 5:21) that he might adopt us as his own? We must be clear here lest our confession become idolatrous and superstitious, anxious and moralistic.

The corporate practice of confession teaches us to see. It teaches us to see ourselves in the light of God's action and promise. The practice of confession is practice in the banishment of

66

illusion, of self-deception, of dishonesty. It is practice in honesty, in telling the truth. The words we use here in public serve as a barrier against the practice of deceit, hypocrisy, and self-deception by which we hide ourselves from God, from our neighbor, from ourselves.

Together and aloud we confess our sins by name. These are *our* sins we confess. We are not here describing someone else. We sometimes encounter the temptation to confess someone else's sin—to deflect attention away from ourselves. We must take care not to do this here. We are concerned here with the "beam" in our own eye, not with the large or small speck in the eye of our neighbor. We must be watchful lest we transform our confession into a secret boast: I thank God I am not as others are. The form of our confession is properly, Lord be merciful to me, a sinner.

B. Confession and Truthfulness

What does it mean for our lives in the world that we, when we gather in the *ekklesia*, confess our sins? How does this liturgy form a style of life? Who do we make ourselves out to be in and through this action?

In the act of confession, we become those who "see clearly"[2] both ourselves and the world in which we are implicated. This clarifying of our perception occurs, let us remember, in the light of the hoped-for liberation. It is as we hope that we see clearly all that contradicts this hope. Adhering to God's promise does not mean we become blind to all that contradicts this promise in the

---

2. That faith produces the capacity to "see clearly" is stressed by Karl Barth in his commentary *The Epistle to the Romans* (London: Oxford University Press, 1933), pp. 46, 156, 309, and *passim*.

world and in ourselves, but that we see this contradiction all the more clearly—in the light of that promise. It is as we hope for freedom that bondage comes more clearly into view. It is because we hope for justice that injustice is seen more starkly. It is in the light of a promised peace that enmity stands out sharply. Hope is not a sedative that tranquilizes us in the face of the world's pain, brokenness, and bondage. It is instead that which *for the first time* genuinely awakens us to our situation. It is because we know that God intends to liberate us and his world, and because we know the cost of that liberation (the cross) that bondage and brokenness become apparent to us, and abhorrent to us.

The confession of sins is the point at which we identify the ways we need and require that which God promises for us and for the world. In the confession of sin, we act out this awareness. Thus, indirectly, we describe ourselves as those who were blind but are now beginning to see.

In this seeing we also engage in naming. One of the features of the exorcisms Jesus performed in the Gospel of Mark was that he knew the demons by name. In naming them he exercised his dominion over them— much as in naming the animals Adam exercised dominion over them. But this dominion is different as its subject is different. Naming the demons is an act of exorcism. Jesus calls the demons by name and so casts them out. In giving his disciples power over sickness, over demons, over sin, Jesus gives them this same authority to name and cast out.

Can we recognize the importance of this power in our lives? Do we not in our world have ample evidence of the power of naming? We all know from our newspapers how totalitarian governments gain power by naming themselves the voice of the people, or the "defenders of freedom." Whether of the left or of the right these regimes destroy freedom in the name of freedom, enslave people in the name of the people. So long as we use the wrong names for things, we cannot hope for freedom or justice. I can call women "girls" and persuade myself they are really immature. I can call human beings "mankind" and subconsciously assume that women are slightly less than (or more than) human. Names have power. They have the power to hold in bondage, to destroy and maim. If you don't believe that, ask any black American.

It is also true in our lives as individuals. If we tell ourselves that things are going well in our marriage—when they are not—chances are we won't do anything to make things better until it is too late. If we tell ourselves that we are tired when we are depressed we may sleep instead of exercising—and get more depressed. Much of psychotherapy is involved in helping people name their fears, their memories, their hopes, their feelings, their relationships. With the wrong names we can't deal appropriately with ourselves or with one another.

Confession is practice in naming. It calls brokenness "brokenness" and bondage "bondage." It makes no room for excuses or for circumlocutions: "We have not loved thee with all our heart and soul and mind and strength, and . . . we have not loved one another as Christ hath loved us." "We have resisted thy Spirit." "We have neglected thy Word and ordinances." "We acknowledge our disobedience and ingratitude, our pride and willfulness, our heedlessness and indifference." "We have allowed self to blind us, pains to embitter us." "Our hearts are divided, crossed by doubts and guilty desires."[3] These are the words we

3. These confessional formulas are found in many Protestant liturgies. I have selected them from *The Book of Worship* (Nashville: The United Methodist Publishing House, 1964), pp. 171-74.

use. They are not just pious phrases. They say who we really are.

We actually do say these things about ourselves, aloud and in public. Who do we become in this action? We become those who have nothing left to hide. Do we seriously imagine there is something worse than this we could admit to? We have violated God's love for us. Is there something more serious than that? We have neglected our neighbor, we have harbored resentment; we know that this is already murder according to Jesus (Matt. 5:21-22). We have said these things. Have we paid attention to what we are saying?

Let us remember why we have said them. We have said them because we know they can no longer separate us from the love of God. We need not hide them. We have said them because they are true. There is no point in hiding the truth. We have said them because God justifies the ungodly and forgives the sinner. We will not pretend that we have no use for this forgiveness and justification—we do not wish to exclude ourselves from this help and hope.

We say these things, admit these things, acknowledge these things. What then? Shall we go back to concealing the truth from ourselves and from one another? If here in public with our neighbors and before God we have said clearly that we are broken and bound, shall we then seek to hide ourselves from our neighbors, our sisters and brothers? How is it possible that we confess our sins and still hide our doubts, our fears, our failures, our guilt, our anxiety from one another? How is it possible to engage in confession and live behind masks? Have we not yet learned that confession leads to forgiveness, that truth leads to freedom? Do we still lock ourselves in the prisons of pretense? Are we so much in love with our chains?

To engage in confession, to truly engage in it, is to expose our chains, to hold them up so that they may be struck off. If we refuse to seriously engage in confession, that can only be because we do not want to lose these chains or because we do not believe that they will truly be removed. That is what the Bible calls sin. It is the sin of unbelief.

If we seriously engaged in confession we would become those people who no longer needed to hide from God, from ourselves, from one another. Adam and Eve hid in the garden. God came seeking them. In the end God has sent the Son. Do we wish to hide or to be found? We say we want to be found. That is why we confess our sins. When we are found we are brought into community with those who are empowered to forgive sin, to call the demons by name, to break the chains. That is why we confess our sin together, aloud, in public. And as we do so we become persons who let go of masks, pretense, hypocrisy. Our lives become an open book. Not because our lives are without sin, but because that sin is being overcome through exposure to the light.

As those who are growing increasingly aware of our sin we are also growing increasingly aware of our neighbors' boundness and brokenness. We confess together. And so we see one another. But this seeing is quite different from what it has been. Formerly our vision of the neighbor was distorted by "the beam in our own eye." It was distorted by our blindness to our own bondage and brokenness—our sin. Then we were offended by our neighbor's sin. We saw it as separating us from them. Our vision was "I thank God that I am not as others are." But in the joint confession of sins we see differently. We see the sin of the other as the occasion for God's mercy and so for our mercy as well. We see the other no longer as   71 the object of condemnation and accusation. We see the other as one like us in need of mercy. Karl Barth writes, "It is as and when we know we are sinners that we know we are brothers."[4]

The confession of sins is the beginning of compassion. We share with our neighbor the need of liberation. The symptoms of this may vary but the need is the same. Sins may vary but sin is common to all. Through the confession of sins we acknowledge our common need, our common brokenness, our common disfigurement, our common paralysis and bondage. Once this has happened we will not wish to exclude from our fellowship and friendship those who are sinners. We will not want to accuse them, blame them, stand over against them. There is nothing in them alien to us. If we had not heard the gospel, if we had not seen the cross, we might still persuade ourselves that others could fall and we still be left standing. But we have heard, we have seen. If the other is condemned how will we stand? we who have heard the gospel yet daily live in unbelief (we have confessed this—let us not now deny it).

Too quickly we search for a way out of this recognition. After all, we have confessed, they have not. Let us suppose this to be true even though it is not self-evident. If we have confessed, then we have recognized and recognize more each day how great is our need for liberation. Does this place us then in a position to separate ourselves from those who also need this liberation? But more, we have confessed because we have hope of liberation. If the others have not confessed, why is this? Is it perhaps because they do not have this hope? And how are they to have such a hope if they do not receive concretely from

4. Barth, *Epistle to the Romans*, p. 101.

us the love and liberation they may have ceased to hope for? And if they do not receive this from us, then on whose head is their sin? And do we have the temerity to accuse them, judge them, condemn them? We who pray, "Forgive us as we have forgiven. . . . " It is quite impossible.

Of course sin remains sin, brokenness is still brokenness, bondage is yet bondage. They must be named, exposed for what they are. But how is this to be done? Can it really be done by accusation and blame? No. Accusation and blame are the marks of the Fall. When, according to the story of Genesis 3, God confronted Adam and Eve, they began to accuse each other. This accusation and blame is the way of imprisonment, not liberation.[5] The naming of bondage and brokenness can only be done by our confessing our sin. This is what we do when we worship together. We name our condition. We model or exemplify this self-knowledge. We invite one another to engage in this self-knowledge and to share in this hope of liberation. We model confession and we embody compassion. Only in this way will the demons be named and cast out.

C. Unmasking the Idols

We need to go further and ask more concretely how this action forms a way of being in the world outside the church. We live in a culture that thrives on illusion, pretense, and masking. We participate all too willingly in these illusions. We live in a world that persuades itself that greater amounts of goods engender greater

---

5. For an illuminating discussion of the Fall that also emphasizes the role of accusation and blame, see Jacques Ellul, *To Will and to Do* (Philadelphia: Pilgrim Press, 1969), pp. 5-58.

happiness, that more weapons mean more security, that it is our right to control the earth's resources, that human rights are luxuries, that justice is dispensed by the privileged and proud, that the end of communism (or capitalism) is the beginning of a new age, that the ends justify the means, that life is less important if it is clothed in skin of a different color or speaks a different tongue or worships in a different way. We are bombarded by these and many more illusions every day.

Practice in confession is practice in penetrating illusion, in unmasking idols, in exposing pretense. In the confession of sin, we do this where it is most difficult—in ourselves. People who seriously practice confession are gaining clarity about their situation. We fall prey to illusion because we want to be fooled. But when we can no longer fool ourselves we are less likely to be fooled in general.

The practice of confession then produces in us a clarity that resists illusion. We will not pretend that we are completely without illusion. That is the worst form of illusion. Have we no longer the need to confess our sins, to unmask our own illusions? We do not yet see with "apocalyptic lucidity." But we have begun to see. And with seeing we gain the capacity to speak, to name the demons, to call illusion "illusion."

If this is true then it means that the Christian is able to unmask the illusions in which our world cloaks itself. Unfortunately, Christians have too often earned for themselves the reputation of clinging to illusions. Nothing could be more catastrophic, for Christians have reason to know that illusion imprisons while truth makes free (John 8:32).

It is an irony then that exposing illusion, self-deception, and ideology has so often in our recent history been undertaken by those outside the church: Freud, Marx, even Nietzsche were above all committed to the task of exposing illusion. This is indeed the critical task of the human sciences. Too often the church has felt uncomfortable under this penetrating gaze. We need not, for we too are heirs of the prophetic tradition. And though we have not yet been divested of all illusion—still we gain practice in this exposure and clarity through the confession of sins.

We live in a world shaped by the illusion that a better standard of living makes us happier. We are continually bombarded with messages that entice us to spend more on ourselves, to acquire more goods, to "live better." We are ensnared by our goods. And all the while this illusion distracts us from the truth, for it is the truth that our standard of living leaves the other and greater part of the world in abject poverty. We become wealthier and they become poorer. We do not even see that we are wealthy, for the seductive vision of "more" and "better" convinces us that we are, after all, only "middle class." Do we dare to call this illusion and deception by its true name?

We live in a world shaped by the illusion that security lies in the threat of violence—that ultimate security lies in the power to apply the ultimate violence. With enough nuclear power to destroy every man, woman, child, every farm, village, and city not once but several times, are we more secure? As time passes more nations reach for this power and actually acquire it. Soon it will be in the grasp of every embittered and lunatic dictator and terrorist. Are we more secure? Our fear leads us to amass more power. Their fear leads them to do the same; until the day comes when our fear shall turn to terror at the final horror of this century of horrors. Do we dare to call this illusion and deception by its true name? There are even those who think it not only possible but right in the name of the Prince of Peace to unleash this madness on the earth! Great is the power of untruth.   75

Only if we see clearly the power of sin in our own lives will we be able to say clearly how sin is present in the world in which we live. Isaiah's commission as a prophet, as one who is called to speak the truth, begins with his confession, "Woe is me . . . for I am a man of unclean lips, and I dwell in the midst of a people of unclean lips" (Isa. 6:5). That Isaiah sees his own bondage to deception and untruth (unclean lips) is the necessary starting point for his role as a speaker of truth. It is when we see how anxiety and fear, guilt and blame rule over our own lives that we begin to be able to see how this anxiety and fear rule the world about us. In the naming of the one, we gain the power to name the other.

In our era when ideology and self-deception have such murderous consequences—when an unlimited technology may be placed at the disposal of any lie or half-truth—it is imperative that we regain the habit of serious confession. As we do so we learn to act in ways that name, expose, and so cast off the demonic sources of bondage in our own hearts, in our community, in our nation, in our world. The confession of sins is therefore an act of freedom.[6]

We name and expose bondage, brokenness, untruth not because we are cynical about ourselves or our world, but because we have hope. Indeed, in a world perched precariously on the brink of lunatic self-destruction it may be that there is only hope if we learn to see through the illusions. Confession is born of hope. Confession may also be our only hope.

It is no mere idle exercise to which we are summoned when in our liturgy we are invited and summoned to confess our sins.

---

6. As Bonhoeffer also notes, "Confession is not a law, it is an offer of divine help for the sinner," *Life Together* (New York: Harper & Brothers, 1954), p. 117.

Repentance

6

What makes true confession so difficult is that we so often call our disease, health; our disfigurement, beauty; our anxiety, happiness; our bondage, freedom. We may indeed have nothing to lose but our chains, but we have grown fond of our chains. They have become a part of us. We confuse them with ourselves. Thus finding ways of naming our chains as chains is an important step toward liberation.

A. The Renunciation of Bondage

In the liturgy we go beyond this naming. We actually turn away from this bondage. We could not do this if we did not know that it was bondage, bondage to the law of sin and death. Without confession we could not repent, but with confession we begin to turn away, to repent, to renounce the chains—including those to which we had become attached.

We turn away. It is important to know this. If we did not turn away then our confession would become simply a new form of self-preoccupation. Confession without repentance is a wallowing in our guilt and shame. We all know of persons for whom confession is a kind of perverse narcissism. Narcissism because it focuses on the self; perverse because it focuses on the blemishes of the self. Sometimes we speak of such persons as having a negative self-image. That term is too mild. It is more often a kind of neurotic self-examination that is fascinated, hypnotized with what is unacceptable about oneself.

We do not confess in order to clutch our guilt to ourselves, in order to be self-preoccupied, for self-preoccupation is the sin of pride. This is true even if this self-preoccupation takes the form of self-accusation, of neurotic guilt, of self-hatred. Pride and despair are two sides of the same coin. They are the two sides of what Luther called "the heart turned inward upon itself."

We confess in order to turn away from that bondage and brokenness with which we have identified ourselves. We confess in order to repent.

This turning away is often very difficult and quite painful. After all, the particular forms bondage takes in our lives are usually very much a part of who we think we are. We know how difficult it is to break habits. Yet that is a very minor thing compared to what is here in view. Let me use an illustration from the area of interpersonal relationships. We may recognize that we regularly attempt to control and possess the people we love: children, lovers, spouses. We may recognize that this is ultimately destructive both of ourselves and of those we love. We may even learn that it has a name, "concupiscence," and that it is regarded by many Christian theologians since Augustine as the most deadly of all sins. We may see that it is the root of much violence and violating of people. All of this is true. I believe all of us experience this form of bondage. All of us are afraid of losing those we love. Not all of us engage in rape and murder but we all live with the same form of bondage, which produces these violent manifestations of the desire to utterly possess the

78

other.[1] But what if we actually set about renouncing this way of being with those we love? We need love in order to live. Can we actually let go of those we love? To do so is like dying—for we risk losing what we need in order to live.

This is only one illustration from among the many that might be mentioned here. But what all of them have in common is that when we get serious about repenting of sin we go through a kind of death. In the Gospel of Mark, Jesus tells his disciples repeatedly that they must lay down their lives in order to really live. If we permit ourselves to see the depth and radicality of our bondage we will see that we must die to what we had thought was life in order to be free, in order to live. Paul can also speak of this as dying to the world (Gal. 6:14), or dying to the flesh (Rom. 8:13). When Paul says this he does not mean some form of asceticism. He means that we seriously turn away from that within us (flesh) and about us (world) that holds us in captivity to anxiety, to enmity, to lovelessness and lifelessness. All of this we must die to. All of this must be renounced. Life must struggle against death, the spirit of life against death, the life of the spirit against flesh.

What is this flesh? Often this has been badly misunderstood. Flesh is not the body. It is the interior rule of sin.[2] It is anxiety about life, it is that anxiety which expresses itself in religion as well as elsewhere. Paul understands that even religion is "flesh," that is, it

---

1. For a further discussion of human sexuality, see my essay "Theological Perspectives on Sexuality" in *The Journal of Pastoral Care* 33 (March 1979):3-16.
2. For Rudolf Bultmann's discussion of the "flesh" in the theology of Paul, see his *Theology of the New Testament*, v. 2 (New York: Charles Scribner's Sons, 1951), pp. 232-46.

is the works of the law by which we attempt to please or to placate God. All this is "flesh" because it grows out of unbelief—out of a refusal to accept the pure grace of God. Flesh for Paul is not skin and bones, it is our life without and against God. That is the life the Spirit opposes. That is the life to which we must die if we are to live. That is the bondage that must be broken if we are to be truly liberated. And this means that life in Christ entails the death of the life that opposes Christ. Our new life means the death of our old life.

Repentance then is like dying. It is a struggle against all that we have known as life. It is a turning away from the pseudo-life we have possessed and toward the true life we are being given. In the next chapter we will explore this a bit more. We turn away in order to turn toward. We do not put our old life to death because of some morbid fascination with death, we participate in the death of Christ in order to share in his life. Repentance is not an end in itself, it is a step toward freedom and life. But it is an exceedingly painful and costly step. It is like dying. We have become so dependent on our chains we fear we shall not be able to live without them.

Sin is not only a power that pervades our lives and world. It also has concrete and specific manifestations. In confession we have not only confessed our sin but also our sins. And in repentance we renounce the specific forms this bondage has taken in our lives. We renounce the envy, which is a symptom of our hatred of the neighbor. We renounce the impatience, which is a symptom of our anxiety. We renounce the specific distortions of our lives in the private and public "thought, word, and deed." We do this not because of some pettiness on our part—a kind of fastidiousness of conscience. It is not because of a breach of religious or moral or legal etiquette that we repent. We repent of that which we see to be the manifestation of bondage, which threatens to overwhelm us and our world. Of course if we do not see these acts, words, and thoughts in that light we can scarcely repent of them. And we can only see them in that light if we have heard the gospel of liberation and have seen the radicality and comprehensiveness of the promised liberation. We need to remember this when we feel impatient with people who do not repent (including ourselves). Where there is no gospel there can be no repentance either in general or in particular.

But we do repent, we do turn away, we do renounce the bondage and brokenness pervasive in our lives alone and in the world. It is important that we do this together and in public. First, because in this way we begin to learn what it is to renounce, to turn away, to "truly and earnestly repent." The public repentance is the model, the demonstration, the blueprint, the paradigm, of our "continual repentance." How are we to learn how to repent without this demonstration and this practice?

The second reason we repent in the service of worship is that we cannot really do it alone. We cannot renounce the bondage of self-preoccupation by ourselves. We have not the strength for it. We can do this only in companionship with those who share in this struggle, whose presence with us is a concrete reminder that we are not alone but are assembled into the Body of Christ. Our repentance is our participation in the death of Christ begun in baptism. But it is as the Body of Christ that we participate in his death. It is as the Body of Christ that we turn away from sin. We cannot do it otherwise. If we could have done it otherwise there would have been no need of the Incarnation.

But the incarnation and crucifixion and   *81*

resurrection of Jesus have taken place. Therefore we are able to act through participating in his action. The people Christ has called to freedom, therefore, in their public action together, renounce the allure of bondage and death. That is why repentance is a part of our liturgy.

B. The Life of Renunciation

What does it mean for our life in the world that in our liturgy we "do truly and earnestly repent of our sins which by thought, word, and deed we have committed"? Is this something we do only in church? If so it is not something we can do in the community of Jesus Christ. We cannot participate in his dying in a stained-glass temple, for he did not die there but in the world, outside the gates, in public view.

Our repentance in the liturgy of the *ekklesia* forms a way or style of life in the world. It is the style of renunciation, the public renunciation of bondage, the turning away from the internal and external powers of repression and oppression.

This is most difficult both to say and to do. We have largely lost any sense of the positive meaning of renunciation. We live, after all, in a consumer society. We teach ourselves to aspire after more consumption, greater benefits, more self-indulgence. The life of self-denial means for us an outmoded way of life practiced by those who secretly or openly hate themselves and the world. It conjures in our minds visions of self-flagellation, sleeping on beds of nails, walking about covered with sackcloth and ashes. How are we to live this sort of life? It is simply preposterous.

That is one side of it. There is another side. Our world of consumption is also a world of cruel asceticism. That seems strange, but look

82

at it. We keep ourselves continually on the move, continually at work. We even work at our "leisure." We are compulsively busy, denying ourselves times of quiet, of serenity. We have forgotten how to feast. We seem to be continually on some sort of diet. We renounce, today, almost everything as carcinogenic. Our society may be characterized both by the pursuit of happiness and by the absence of joy. It is not only fasting we no longer understand but feasting as well. The ancient church knew perfectly well that you can't feast without fasting, that there is no joy without renunciation, that there is no liberty which is not a turning away from bondage. The church also knew that fasting and renunciation and repentance are not an end in themselves—they are a preparation for the feast of joy and freedom.

Renunciation is one of the characteristics of a life of freedom. It is one of the ways we signal freedom from compulsion, from self-indulgence, from consumption, from anxiety and fear. In this light we may learn to appreciate the public demonstration of renunciation characteristic of the monastic life. Those entering this vocation took at least three vows: poverty, chastity, and obedience. By understanding something of the meaning of these vows as well as their limitations, we may gain some sense of the possible forms of renunciation for our lives—for lives committed not to monasticism, but to some other form of Christian vocation.

These three vows have in common that they strike at the heart of the ways we habitually try to give our lives meaning apart from and over against God. They are an assault therefore on bondage. They are, in their true meaning and intention, a demonstration of freedom.

The vow of poverty demonstrates freedom from the ways we seek to protect our lives from scarcity. We try to give our lives meaning by accumulating and consuming things. We try to insure our lives in the world, to protect them. We store up "treasure." We do this with our bank accounts, our houses, our life insurance. And the result is not less but more anxiety about our lives. There is never enough, so we walk a treadmill of ever increasing acquisition and expenditure. We have a standard of living to maintain, or to achieve. We are prisoners of our goods. We are not free to "sell all that we have and give to the poor." We are bound hand and foot. Like hostages we identify with our captors. We fall in love with our chains.

The vow of poverty is an act of freedom—a refusal of this bondage, a turning away from this prison, from these chains. It is doing this in public. It makes us a bit nervous to see people choose poverty. We are not speaking here of the poor but of those who choose to be poor—for the sake of the gospel. Being poor because one is born poor and prevented from being anything else is not freedom but bondage. That many are poor we tend to take for granted. But that one should actually choose poverty—that does bother us. It exposes our bondage to our own standard of living. It is an assault on the world's bondage to the chains of acquisition and consumption.

The vow of chastity and celibacy may strike us as even more strange than the vow of poverty. Especially in Protestant circles we tend to think of this as an entirely unnatural denial of sexuality. The only exception we habitually make in this regard is for homosexuals, who we quite readily assume should be celibate. That in itself shows how far we are from a proper understanding of the vocation of celibacy. Indeed it shows how far we are from an understanding of marriage as a Christian vocation.[3]

But what is the point of celibacy? Let us consider what we take for granted: the nature of marriage and family. We may dimly remember that the New Testament has very little good to say about marriage. Of course many of us discount Paul's view that it is better to marry than to be consumed (I Cor. 7:9). That rather unflattering view of marriage and family life is easily explained away. But what do we make of Jesus renouncing his own family and calling those who would follow him to do the same (Mark 3:31-35; 10:29-30)? That is more difficult to explain.

If we were to consider marriage and family quite soberly we might be forced to admit there is much bondage here, much lack of freedom. To what extent is marriage a way of claiming possession and ownership over another person? To what extent do we marry and stay married in order to keep loneliness at bay—in order to assure ourselves of someone who will conjure away our solitude? (It doesn't work very well: Bernard Shaw defined marriage as the maximum of loneliness with the minimum of privacy.) To what extent do we use the other person to enhance our own prestige—to live in the reflected beauty or power or respectability of the other? And what of our children? To what extent is their achievement used to reassure us that we are, after all, good parents? And what is all of this but enslavement? For marriage and family are, all too often, merely the use of other people for our own ends—

---

3. For further discussion of this point, see my "Homosexuality and Christian Faith" in *The Christian Century* 94 (February 16, 1977):137-42. This article is republished in *Homosexuality and the Christian Faith: A Symposium*, ed. Harold Twiss (Valley Forge, Pa.: Judson Press, 1978) and in *Homosexuality and Ethics*, ed. Edward Bachelor (Philadelphia: Pilgrim Press, 1980).

enslaving and ensnaring them and ourselves in this vicious melodrama of prestige and power, of jealousy and manipulation.

The vow of celibacy is a renunciation of all this. It is a refusal to establish one's own existence through this most intimate form of bondage. It is doing this in public. As such it is a public witness and demonstration of freedom. It is a reminder that our lives are not determined by manipulating others—that it is possible to let go of all that. Indeed it is precisely the vow of celibacy that makes the vow of marriage also possible as a free and responsible vocation. I really believe that only if we can do without marriage and family can we freely live with and within them. The vow of celibacy then is a refusal of the easy consolations of an unreflective marriage. It is a sign of freedom; of freedom to love all equally. At its best it is not a denial of or repression of sexuality but a sign of the transformation, the sublimation, of sexuality into love of the neighbor.

The vow of obedience is similarly difficult for us. To obey another is to surrender one's own quest for authority and prestige. It is to let go of that quest, to renounce it in favor of obedience to another. This again is not the obedience of the slave to the master. It is not a "natural obedience." It has nothing in common, for example, with the view that women simply as women ought to be obedient to their husbands. Enforced rather than chosen obedience is bondage rather than freedom. This is instead the choice of obedience, the free and sovereign renunciation of self-will. (Traditionally one obeys those who themselves have taken this vow—this is what distinguishes it from the obedience of slave to master.) This vow only makes sense if it is made by those who are free. These are the ones who *choose* to obey, to serve. It is when these choose obedience that the obedience is a sign of freedom and is a renunciation of bondage.

C. Renunciation and Freedom

The vows of poverty, celibacy, and obedience are the traditional ways many Christians have institutionalized renunciation as a style of life. Of course we know only too well that these can readily become a new form of bondage, that they can enshrine spiritual pride, repression, and oppression. This is why the reformers, in turn, renounced these vows. Renouncing the vows was for them also a demonstration of freedom, not a self-indulgence, not a surrender to internal or external necessity. What is it for us?

We may protest that we are in any case not going to become nuns or monks. I do not wish to encourage people to do this at all. The point of considering these vows is to see in them illustrations of what it means to renounce bondage—in the world, in the intimate sphere of relations, even in the self. We do not need to adopt these specific forms of renunciation. Repentance cannot be repentance if it is not an act of freedom rather than law. But how are we to display this freedom in our lives? What are the elements of renunciation we can make a part of our manner of living?

Any answer to this question requires close attention to our lives and to the concrete and specific forms our bondage takes. This is not the sort of thing for which we can write a general prescription. It must be an act of freedom—a refusal of bondage rather than acceptance of bondage. We need to ask quite soberly, What are the ways we are enslaved to our own whims, desires, self-gratifications? (Some of us will have to ask, How are we preoccupied with guilt and fear?) This will give us a place to begin renunciation. We may go on to ask about the specific forms of bondage in our relationships. How do we ensnare others or persuade others to ensnare us? How do we 87 use other people (or get them to use us)? That too may give us ample scope for designing concrete forms and expressions of renunciation in our lives.

But beyond that is the public sphere of our lives in the world. What are the public forms of oppression and bondage we unconsciously or consciously collaborate in? Are there not ample ways to enact a public refusal of these structures? What of the continual incitement to acquiring and consuming? What of the continued insistence on efficiency at the expense of people? What of the ways our society protects itself from the sight of the sick and dying, of the old or the "crazy," of the criminal or the disfigured? What of the ways we insure our standard of living by exploiting the Third World or the poor in our streets? What of the ways we gain security through stockpiling weapons, which will certainly destroy all of us one day? Are there here some points at which it is possible for us to engage in public renunciation? I think much offers itself here for our action.

Perhaps too much. We can begin to feel over-whelmed by the magnitude of self-destructiveness and inhumanity in our world. We may sabotage ourselves by asking, But what can I hope to accomplish? The answer of course is—nothing. But if we believe that God has acted in Christ to redeem his world then what we are to do is to point to, to signify, to demonstrate that redemption. Our renunciation does not create freedom. Rather, it is created by freedom and points to freedom. It is a sign, a liturgy in the world, a dramatic gesture. It is the way we testify about overcoming the principalities and powers, which was inaugurated in Christ's death and resurrection.

Renunciation is a sign of hope. Our world desperately needs such a sign. To us it is given to be such a sign: the salt, the yeast, the light, the city set upon a hill. Without such a sign, our world is without hope.

Prayer for Pardon 7

I n repentance we turn from bondage in order to
turn toward freedom. The prayer for pardon is the
liturgical action that represents and exemplifies
this turn toward freedom. In it we turn toward
the healing and deliverance God has promised and
executed in Christ. It is this turning toward that gives
precision and clarity and force to our turning away. In
dying to the world, we turn away not from the world
in general but from the world as it resists, or is
incompatible with, that reign of justice and love toward
which we turn. In "dying to the self," we turn away not
from ourselves in general but from that in us which
resists or is incompatible with that freedom and joy
toward which we turn.

A. Turning Toward God

In the prayer for pardon, we turn toward God,
toward the one who has come to us and will come to us
in Jesus the liberator. We turn toward God in order to
ask God to turn toward us in mercy and in pardon.
Without this turning toward, our turning away from
bondage and brokenness would be in vain. It is that
toward which we turn that prevents our renunciation
from being petty or arbitrary. We turn toward
freedom and deliverance for the world—
therefore our renunciation of the world is not

a turning *against* the world but a turning *for* the world, for its freedom and ours.[1]

If our renunciation had no such point or aim it would be circular. We would find ourselves like those lost in the wilderness whose way never advances but only returns upon itself. Jesus told the story of the "unclean spirit" (Matt. 12:43-45; Luke 11:24-26) who departs from a person, then returns with "seven other spirits more evil than himself" to dwell in the one from whom the first had departed, "and the last state of that man becomes worse than the first." If we think only to renounce the evil, our lives are only "empty, swept, and put in order." Thus moral rectitude is an open invitation to infinitely greater bondage than we have known before. It is not in renouncing evil alone but in turning toward a positive freedom that bondage is truly broken. We know only too well that an existence which only renounces sin may become self-righteous, anxious, legalistic—in short—a worse bondage. We do not only turn away from bondage therefore, we turn toward freedom.

How do we execute this turn? We do not have to have recourse to a theory of the possibility of such an action. For we in fact execute this turn in our liturgy. We pray, "Lord, have mercy on us." We say, "Pardon and deliver us from all our sins." With these words we turn toward God, toward God's future, toward freedom.

We turn toward God. This is the most obvious yet

---

1. Thus Paul can claim that "the creation waits with eager longing for the revealing of the sons of God . . . because the creation itself will be set free from its bondage to decay and obtain the glorious liberty of the children of God" (Rom. 8:19, 21). In this way it is made clear that our deliverance is not a condemnation of the world but part of a global, universal deliverance.

perhaps also the most astonishing feature of our prayer. We who know that we are without God turn toward God. We who have identified ourselves as godless and godforsaken, we who know we are sinners, nevertheless do actually turn toward God. This is certainly an audacious and presumptuous move. In this prayer for pardon, as in all our prayer, we address ourselves to God. We do not and cannot do this on the basis of who we are, for we have already said we are sinners. Rather our turning toward God is based on who God is: "Whose property is always to have mercy."

We turn then not to an anonymous supreme being but to that God who has come to us in Jesus the Liberator. It is because we know, in advance, that God has turned toward us that we turn toward God. "While we were yet sinners," Paul writes, "Christ died for us" (Rom. 5:8). At this point we do not need to explore theories of atonement or of the nature and person of Christ. At this point all we require is to see that the language of faith claims that our bondage and brokenness, our godlessness and godforsakenness, has already been invaded by God in such a way as to make it possible for us to turn to God.

We turn to God asking God for pardon and deliverance. We do this simply because God has promised us pardon and deliverance, a promise affirmed and ratified in Christ who is, as Paul says, "the 'Yes' to all of God's promises" (II Cor. 1:20 GNB). We therefore do not turn with hesitation and uncertainty, but confidently and boldly. We who have no claim nevertheless make this claim in the name and for the sake of Jesus.

What does it mean to ask God for mercy, pardon, and deliverance? For what are we asking when we ask for this? We are not here asking for something God might or might not give. We 91 are asking God to be God. It is easy to miss the importance of this—to suppose that we are asking for one among many possible things, that we seek here one from among several possible gifts or favors. That is not what is at stake in this petition. We are asking God who *is* merciful *to be* merciful. We are asking that God be God in such a way as to be God for us and with us. The prayer for pardon, like the petitions—"Hallow your name, your kingdom come, your will be done"—asks God to be God for us.

The prayer for pardon is then the audacious claim that God be for us who God has promised and declared himself to be. Rightly does Calvin speak of the presumptuousness of prayer![2] And rightly do we ask this, in the name of Jesus. The Christian community confesses its faith that in Jesus, God has indeed already come to us.

That we who are sinners ask God to come to us means that we ask God to come to us in mercy. We who are against God ask God to be for us. We therefore ask for pardon. We who are bound and collaborate in our own bondage ask God for deliverance. The coming of God means deliverance. The reign and rule of God means that the blind see, the lame walk, the captives are freed, the dead are raised. It means the abolition of sorrow and of death, of injustice and oppression. We ask this God to come and so we ask for this deliverance.

But this deliverance comes not for the individual alone. God is no guardian angel but the Creator and Lord of the universe. To ask this God for deliverance is

---

2. Calvin, *Institutes* III. XX.12. This characteristic of prayer is emphasized by Jesus in the story of the importunate friend (Luke 11:5-8) and of the importunate widow (Luke 18:1-8).

to ask for a universal deliverance of God's world from the dominion of principalities and powers. To pray to this God for pardon and deliverance is not to ask God to deal with our private and "spiritual" needs alone but with the desperate needs of God's world. It is because God "so loved the world" (John 3:16) that we know that liberating love to be directed toward us. To ask God to deliver us means as well that we ask God to deliver the world. We cannot ask for pardon and deliverance while still wishing that some be kept in bondage. To seek deliverance and pardon of *this* God is to seek deliverance and pardon for all people.

We say and sing, "Lamb of God, who takes away the sins of *the world*, have mercy on *us*." We ask for the mercy promised to all to be given to us as well. It is because God delivers the world that God delivers us.

To turn toward God in prayer for pardon and deliverance means then that we turn in earnest desire for the liberty of God's whole creation. We turn in our prayer toward freedom. It is this desire and yearning for freedom that gives clarity to our turn from bondage.

To summarize then, in our prayer for pardon our turning away from bondage receives its goal, aim, and direction. It becomes a turning toward God. It asks that God turn toward us and come to us in mercy and pardon and therefore with liberation. The liberation we yearn for is real and radical liberation—it is the liberation that only comes from God. But because it comes from *this* God, who created heaven and earth, it is a liberation for the whole earth and all who dwell therein. Because we seek this general deliverance (the kingdom of God) we also seek particular and concrete deliverance (the forgiveness of sins).

The assembly (*ekklesia*) comes together to   *93*

act for the sake of the world. One element of this action is the turning toward freedom exemplified in the prayer for pardon.

B. The People Who Yearn for Freedom

Who do we declare ourselves to be in this action? In public and together we call for God to come to us, in mercy and pardon, with deliverance. We define ourselves as those who yearn for God's promised liberation. Of course this means that we need this liberation. That is precisely what we have specified in the confession of sins. We have named the concrete forms of our bondage and brokenness, and we have renounced our collaboration and complicity in this bondage and brokenness.

But now we claim we actually desire this liberation for ourselves and therefore for the world. Nothing could be more contrary to the appearance that many of our churches give of a smug self-satisfaction. Often our churches seem to be bulwarks of the status quo, interested in preserving, and congratulating themselves on, a relatively secure and comfortable way of life. We often appear to be quite content with life as it is, with ourselves as we are. All that seems to worry us is the sign that others may not very much like the way things are—the poor, the minorities, the "new" women, the Third World.

But here in our prayer for pardon we declare ourselves to be supremely dissatisfied with "the way things are." We ask for and even demand a fundamental change in the interior and exterior status quo. Here, if only for a moment, we describe ourselves as those who yearn for freedom. Here, if only for a moment, we speak and act as if we were no different from the woman in a jail cell, or the man who cries "death to the system," or those who hunger and thirst for righteousness, for justice and liberty. Here, if only for a moment, we act as if we are those whom Jesus came to save, to whom he came to announce the Good News.

Are we here only pretending? Is this pure "make believe," mere hypocrisy? Or is the appearance of satisfaction and contentment with ourselves and our world the "make believe"? Is that the pretense, the illusion? Which are we? Upon this question rests the integrity of our worship.

We frequently distinguish between our life in the world and our life in church. Often we call our secular and everyday existence "the real world" implying that that is who we really are. What happens if we turn this around and suppose that who we really are is who we appear to be in worship (not, of course, covered with our Sunday best and polite manners but uncovered in our action and liturgy)? We must ask then, are we as contented with ourselves and our world as we often appear to be? Or are we instead those who deeply yearn for a new heaven and a new earth? It is possible that here in the often sleepy routine of our worship we catch a glimpse of who we really and deeply are?

In the actions here in the corporate worship of the gathered community, we signify not just who we are but, still more, who we are becoming. We publicly demonstrate the life into which we and all God's creation are being summoned. Thus the difference between who we are here and who we appear to be elsewhere is the all-too-apparent difference between the new and the old life, the new and the old world. If this is so then it becomes all the more urgent to ask, How is this new life to take form in our real and everyday world?

C. Solidarity with Those Who Yearn for Freedom

The way we worship can and must shape the way we live. In the prayer for pardon, we express our yearning for deliverance and freedom. We give voice to the common sigh and yearning of the whole creation. We do this neither desperately nor uncertainly, but clearly, confidently, expectantly. How are this attitude and action to be made the shape and form of our life in the world?

We will not be able to separate ourselves from those who yearn for freedom, for in their yearning we will discern echoes of our own yearning. Often we suppose that the aspirations of others are a threat to us. When persons protest their poverty, their exploitation, their exclusion from economic and political processes we may be tempted to see this as a threat to our own position. But when we begin to see clearly our own imprisonment in our "position" and "status" we may see in the protest of the other against this status not a threat but a deliverance. We have become the beneficiaries of these economic and political systems at a great price. The price we have paid is anxiety and fear and resentment. Those who now protest these systems are not enemies but friends, whose protest is an occasion and a call to us to give up our enslavement of them and of ourselves and to join in the common desire and yearning for liberty and justice.

To permit our prayer for pardon to shape our life in the world means then that we join in solidarity with all those who earnestly desire freedom. We may object that all too often these oppressed seem to desire merely a secular or material liberation. There is no doubt much truth in this.

96

But we must also recall that the reign of God we yearn for does not exclude the reign of justice, the overthrow of oppression, the messianic banquet of plenty, and the abolition of human misery—thus those who yearn for these things yearn for a part of what we desire. Indeed the desire for earthly justice is far nearer to a desire for the reign of God than is the smug complacency with the way things are, so characteristic of some of our communities.

We would do well to remember that those who responded gladly to Jesus' message were not those who were comfortable economically, socially, or politically. Those who heard him gladly were those who "had nothing to lose but their chains." In our own day the community of faith grows and exhibits astonishing vitality among those peoples who have been oppressed and who hear in the gospel the echo and indeed the amplification of their yearning for justice and freedom.

There is then some plausibility to the claim made by James Cone that in American society, the black community is the true people of God and that only by identifying with this community in its quest for freedom can white Christians truly worship Christ.[3] If blackness has become for us the symbol of oppression and the symbol of the desire for freedom then it is true that we must become black in order to be Christian. So long as we identify ourselves with "whiteness" as a condition of privilege and of conscious or unconscious exploitation we can never truly yearn for that radical

---

3. This position is effectively maintained in virtually all of James Cone's books and in his essay "Theology as the Expression of God's Liberating Activity for the Poor" in *The Vocation of the Theologian*, ed. Theodore W. Jennings, Jr. (Philadelphia: Fortress Press, 1985), p. 124.

and complete liberation, which is the reign of God. Thus we can never truly desire deliverance and pardon, the coming of the kingdom, or the accomplishment of God's will.

This is why we so desperately need the companionship of those who yearn for deliverance. It is all too easy to forget our own need, desire, and yearning for justice and for an end to death and sorrow. When we separate ourselves from the dying, from the broken and maimed, from the poor and oppressed, we forget the deep heart of desire and yearning that beats within us. Our desire becomes trivial, half-hearted, distracted. We become irritated with those who truly hunger and thirst for justice, or we grow fearful of them. Only in fellowship with those whose minds or bodies are broken, with those who are dying, with those who are imprisoned or oppressed, may we learn again what it is to hunger and thirst for righteousness, to earnestly desire the coming of God, to yearn for deliverance and freedom.

We are, we know, divided in our desire. We both love and hate our condition. We benefit from "the way things are" and we know that we are enslaved by the way things are. We must join Paul when he says, "I do not do the good I want, but the evil I do not want is what I do" (Rom. 7:18-19). It is because and so long as we are thus divided that we need the liturgy of liberation; that we need confession, repentance, prayer for pardon, and forgiveness.

Knowing this may help us to understand our neighbor, our sister or brother with whom we are so apt to become impatient. Are we not often "put off" by the contradictions in the lives of those we know most intimately? Do we not become impatient with the ways they seem to sabotage themselves, to betray themselves, to degrade themselves? Perhaps in our experience with this prayer for pardon we may begin to discover a way of bearing with them. We may begin to discover in ourselves an echo of their yearning for a different and a better life. Of course this yearning is often misdirected both in them and in us, but as we become more aware of our own yearning for deliverance we may find ways of understanding them. We may be able to discern their longing as one with our own, however differently expressed or concealed.

William Lynch has suggested that a great many of us, perhaps all of us, suffer from the inability to hope, desire, or wish.[4] We have spent much of our lives suppressing or denying our hope. We have become baffled about what we really want. After all, do we not continually tell ourselves that our wishing is "unrealistic," that we ought not to "get our hopes up," that in order to prevent disappointment we must give up desire? And do we not then hide from ourselves and from others what we want? The result of this is that we can no longer say to ourselves or to others what we want. Our desire and yearning become mute, and then we are perfect prey for all those who would tell us what we want. We permit ourselves to be bullied into wanting and desiring what does not and cannot meet our yearning or answer our longing. Perhaps this is why we are so busy and such frenetic consumers.

When we pray for pardon and deliverance we become once again those who deeply and earnestly desire. We give voice to longing and yearning. We cry out for a future, for freedom, for help and mercy and compassion. We become those who hope. In becoming those who hope we become like the children Jesus

---

4. William F. Lynch, *Images of Hope* (Baltimore: Helicon, 1965).

blessed, saying, "For to such belongs the kingdom of heaven."

And in this hoping, this simple and earnest desiring, we begin already to be free. We begin to be free of that anxiety and fear which inhibits our longing; free of that bondage to confusion which disguises and deflects our desire.

Participating in the prayer for pardon is practice in hope. We need this practice. We need it in order to recognize our need and longing for freedom. We need it in order to recognize in our neighbor the desire for freedom. We need it in order to enter into solidarity with all those who hunger and thirst for justice and freedom, for the righteousness of God.

We participate in the prayer for pardon together to testify publicly about our yearning and desire and so to give our lives shape. We need this solidarity, this mutual encouragement, if we are to grow in the courage to hope.

When we pray for pardon in the liturgy of the *ekklesia* we express the world's need and desire. We express the hope for deliverance, for the coming of God in mercy and with healing. What we do here is to enact our hope as a hope for our lives in the world. In so doing we learn to live this hope in and with and for the world.

D. Fruits Worthy of Repentance

The act of confession, repentance, and prayer for pardon is the act of conversion, of turning from the old and toward the new, from bondage toward liberty, from the dominion of sin and death toward the dominion of joy and generosity.

In the New Testament narratives this turn is represented by the figure of John the Baptist. His ministry is the messianic ministry of preparation— preparation for the coming of

God. It is thus appropriate here to reflect on his message and the way in which this message bears on that turn in our lives from the old toward the new, from bondage toward liberation.

To those who come to him in the wilderness to undergo the baptism of repentance, John announces the necessity of "bear[ing] fruits that befit repentance" (Luke 3:8). It is in this way that the turn symbolically made in the rite of purification may be realized in the lives of those who respond to this call.

But what are these "fruits worthy of repentance"? What are the ways our lives may exhibit the reality of this turn from bondage in anticipation of the reign of God? All too often we have understood this phrase in a purely personal and private way, thinking of sin only as interior defects and of repentance only as a private and interior turning. Yet to understand in this way is to defy the biblical word itself, which points in quite a different direction.

When the people ask, "What then shall we do [to exhibit and realize this turn]?" John replies, "He who has two coats, let him share with him who has none; and he who has food, let him do likewise" (Luke 3:11). And when the officials of government ask him the same question he replies, "Collect no more than is appointed you" (Luke 3:13), and when soldiers ask he replies, "Rob no one by violence or by false accusation, and be content with your wages" (Luke 3:14).

The astonishing thing about these replies is that each one points to the public realm of social justice as the place we are to demonstrate and realize this turn from bondage toward liberation. There is no biblical basis whatever for understanding   *101* this turn in a purely religious or private and interior sense. The fruits worthy of repentance are actions of generosity and justice in the public sphere of economics and politics. A refusal of this sphere, a withdrawal into the sphere of the private and interior, is a refusal to turn from bondage toward liberation. When the church focuses its attention away from this public sphere, it sides with the old order of bondage and injustice and oppression. Marx spoke of religion in this sense as "the opium of the people," but John is far harsher: "You brood of vipers," he says to those who substitute religious obligations and moralistic scrupulosity for the authentic demands of repentance.

And what are these demands? Renouncing the false privileges of wealth and position and power and turning toward the poor with compassion, generosity, and justice. The mark of our turn from the old aeon to the new is whether we share all that we have with the poor, whether we abolish the systems that impoverish the people—not only in our own land but of the Third World—whether we refuse the use of violence to victimize those less powerful than ourselves. And this message refers particularly to those of us who are citizens of the wealthy, powerful, and "Christian" nations of the "first world." We become more wealthy while the wretched of the earth sink lower in misery. The institutions that protect our "way of life" place the rest of the world under staggering debt and usurious interest. The forces of national security are employed to terrorize the weak (think of U.S. policy in Nicaragua) in the name of "freedom." The message of John concerning fruits worthy of repentance strikes very close to home.

102   As does his warning of "the wrath to come."

For day by day it becomes ever more clear that economic systems built on greed, and political systems built on violence, can only bring upon themselves the cataclysm of terror, the final holocaust. These images, once confined to prophetic and apocalyptic imagination, have in our time become a menacing reality visible to all. Thus it has become all the more urgent that we and all nations of the earth bring forth fruits worthy of repentance.[5]

Yet we do this not in desperation and fear but in hope and joy. For the new age is already dawning in our world, a dawn announced in the words of assurance and in the pronouncement of pardon.

5. For a discussion of the political character of sin and repentance, see Dorothee Soelle, *Political Theology* (Philadelphia: Fortress Press, 1974).

The Words of Assurance   8

W e pray for pardon and for deliverance. In so doing we turn toward God and ask God to turn toward us. In the words of assurance, which follow our prayer, we hear that this prayer has been heard, that our desire has been and will be met. Our word of desire is met with God's word of promise:

> The Lord redeems the life of his servants; none of those who take refuge in him will be condemned. (Ps. 34:22)
>
> For as the heavens are high above the earth, so great is his steadfast love toward those who fear him; as far as the east is from the west, so far does he remove our transgressions from us. (Ps. 103:11-12)
>
> The saying is sure and worthy of full acceptance, that Christ Jesus came into the world to save sinners. (I Tim. 1:15)

These and many other texts are recited in our liturgy. In them we hear the answer to our hope, the promise that makes our hope possible.

A. God's Word and Ours

In the reading of these texts in our worship, we join with the whole community of faith in hearing and repeating the assurance that the liberation we desire is the liberation desired and promised by God. Indeed in the reading and hearing of these texts, we *become* the community summoned into being by God's word of promise and of commission. The words of assurance are first of all and most obviously the words of Scripture taken from the Old and the New Testaments. They are texts asserting that God promises forgiveness, liberation, and healing. Our "words of assurance" consist of repeating these texts. What does this mean?

It means, first, we are assured by the same words that have assured the community of faith from its beginning and through the centuries. We are addressed as the people of Israel were, and are, addressed and so enter into solidarity with Israel, with its history, its election, its faith, its destiny. We are addressed as the disciples of Jesus and the community of Christians were and are addressed, and so we enter into solidarity with the church, with its commission, its history, its faith, its destiny.

These words have indeed created both Israel and the church. For these words have called them into being, given them life and courage, and summoned them into relation to God and the world. In this sense both Israel and the church are communities of the Word founded and created and sustained by these words.[1] In repeating these words, in speaking and in hearing them, we too are called into being as the people of God, as the people to whom God speaks these words of assurance and promise.

But these are, after all, human words. They are the words that have been spoken and written, read,

---

1. For a more detailed analysis of the language of faith and the meaning of "word of God," see my *Beyond Theism: A Grammar of God-Language* (New York: Oxford University Press, 1985), especially chapters 4 and 12.

repeated, and heard by people like us. Yet we also call
these words "God's Word." This means that in and
through the words we address to one another, God also
addresses us. The human words that articulate the faith
of Israel and the church are also words that bring to
speech God's own address, promise, and Word to us.
These words, or rather the documents containing these
words, are given a special place in the life and liturgy of
the community. They are given this place not because
of some theory of inspiration (these theories only come
much later) but because the community of faith has
found itself to be addressed and called into being by
these words. It recognizes that in these very diverse
texts it has heard and knows that it will hear again not
only the voice of its ancestors in the faith but also that
Word which created faith both for them and for us. This
does not mean that faith is created only by just these
words. There is no word magic here, no secret
incantation. But it does mean that these words have
created faith, and the faith by which we live is not a
different faith from that which is articulated and called
into being also by these words.

B. Words of Promise

The words we repeat here are words of promise.
They are words that speak of reality in the future tense.
They are not then only words *from* the past but words *of*
the future. They remind us of what God *has* done
in order to assure us concerning what God *will* do.
God will have mercy, God will come to us, God will
deliver us.

In order to understand what we mean by
saying that "God promises," it may be helpful

to reflect on what we mean by promising

in our everyday lives.[2] If I say, "I will come to you next Monday," what am I doing? I am first saying something about the future. But is it a promise? If I prefaced this sentence with the words "It is likely that" would it be a promise? It would not. Nor would it be one if I said "It is certain that" or "unlikely that" or "impossible that." In none of these assertions do I commit myself. I only *promise* when I *commit* myself. But what if I said, "I promise that it will rain tomorrow"? That sounds like a promise. But is it? Can it be? Or more exactly can I promise such a thing? I can predict it with more or less accuracy, but a prediction is not a promise. Nor can I appropriately promise that which I cannot deliver. If it doesn't rain tomorrow you would not accuse me of being faithless but of being silly to promise something over which I have no control. To promise then is to commit oneself with respect to that over which one has power—namely oneself.

Let us consider one more aspect of promising. Is there a difference between a promise and a threat? Suppose I say, "I promise you that I will care for you when you are sick." If instead when you are sick I abandon you or take advantage of you, you would rightly conclude that I have not kept my promise—that I am faithless or dishonorable. But what if I said, "I promise you that when you are sick I will abandon you"? This already seems odd, does it not? How odd it is becomes clear if instead of abandoning you I care for you. Am I now faithless? Does it make sense to accuse me of breaking my promise? It seems

---

2. The discussion of promising, which follows, owes a good deal to Ludwig Wittgenstein, *Philosophical Investigations* (3rd. ed.) (New York: Macmillan, 1958) and to J. L. Austin, *Philosophical Papers* (Oxford: Oxford University Press, 1970).

that promising has to do with a benefit conferred upon the one to whom I promise. Threatening does not have the same force as promising.

This may seem to have taken us quite far from our theme. Actually it has brought us nearer to the center of our question. It in fact reminds us of a story Jesus is reported to have told of the son who promised to do as his father commanded and did not and of the son who said he would not do as he was commanded but did. Which of these sons found favor with his father (Matt. 21:28-32)? Jesus was not a language philosopher but he knew something about promising.

There are a great many other things to say about promising, but I will only draw your attention to one more thing. To *promise* is to *act*. When I promise, I do something. Children already know this. That is why they want to know, "Do you promise?" If I say "I will take you to the movie," as a child you may respond, "Promise?" If I say no, or hedge, you will not be content. If I say "I promise" you may very well be content. Why is this? Is it because my promise assures you? Yes, but why does it assure you? It is because it is now not only that I *will* do something (take you to the movies) but *have* done something (promised). It may even be that the promise is what makes the movie important, for when I promise I commit myself to you. That may even be more important than the movie. That might have been what you wanted from me when you asked me to take you to the movie. The movie itself may be only a token of what you really want: that I commit myself to you. When I have done that, I have done no small thing.

We began this reflection on promising by
noting that our words of assurance are words

of promise and by asking, What does it mean to say that God promises? We are now in a much better position to answer that question. To say that God promises must mean that God commits himself to us for our benefit. God does not predict something about the future but commits himself to our future. In doing this God has already done something. The promise is a kind of advance payment on that which is promised.

And what is promised? Just that God will come to us and bring us to himself, not to destroy but to save. God promises us himself. And in promising, God already comes to us precisely in this word of promise. God gives us his Word.[3]

The Christian community has proclaimed that there can be no doubt that God has given the divine Word, for God's Word has become flesh and dwelt among us (John 1:14). Paul says of Jesus that he is the yes and amen to all God's promises (II Cor. 1:20).

When we repeat and hear repeated those "words of assurance" we become and are those to whom God promises himself, those to whom God gives his Word. The repetition of these words is the reiteration of God's promise. In and through these words God gives his Word. That is why they are "words of assurance." They

---

3. In these paragraphs and in other places where I am insisting on the reflexive character of promising (himself, his Word) and on the intimate connection between God and the world (his world), I have resorted to the traditional use of the masculine pronoun for God, which I have otherwise sought to avoid. I apologize for this to those who are rightly sensitive to the "masculinist" bias of this language but I found no other way to stress the reflexive and possessive relationships that would make acceptable English sense without detracting from the main point. This is but a further indication of the tension in relationship between our word and that Word which is God.

assure us because they are the "happening in advance" of that for which we hope. That for which we yearn is already present in these words, for in these words God commits himself to us and so "assures us."

C. Words That Assure

We may now notice a further feature of these words we repeat. We began by noticing that they were words of Scripture taken from documents in the Old and New Testaments. Because this is so we may find ourselves thinking that the language is archaic, the ideas somewhat strange. After all they came to us from the ancient past and so are bound to sound a bit alien to us. They are not the language we would most naturally use to reassure ourselves.

The ancient words precisely by their strangeness remind us of something very important. It is one thing *to reassure* oneself. It is quite different *to be assured* by another. The latter is likely to be more assuring somehow. Why is this? I can always undermine my own assurance by saying, "But I may be mistaken." It is precisely when I have done this that I need to be assured, but then I cannot reassure myself. I need another to assure me. This quite superficial reflection points to a more fundamental reality. We need one another in order to exist. We need to be addressed by another. Alone, I am subject to illusion and to self-deception. I need another in order to be truthful, in order to be free, in order to be assured, in order to be.

The words of assurance are not my own words by which I address myself. They are the words of another by which I am addressed. It is their otherness that makes them appropriate as words of
110 assurance. The very otherness of these words

points to that Other who in and through these words promises himself to us and so assures us.

The words of promise become for us words of assurance. It is in this sense that we may say we are "created" by these words. These words through which God gives his Word bring us into being as people of faith, as the *community of faith*. These words are not only addressed to us, they are also committed to us, entrusted to us. To be or to become the community of the Word is not only to be the community addressed *by* these words but the community that addresses the world *with* these words. We who are "born" from these words are also the "bearers" of these words.

We learn to speak by being spoken to. The ancient words we are addressed by and that we recite here in the liturgy teach us to speak. We learn to speak to one another words of assurance. The words of scripture in general and these words of assurance in particular are entrusted to us for the purpose of becoming the language by which we address one another. By being entrusted to us they do not become a possession that we may hide away or keep to ourselves; words not used become a dead language. They are entrusted to us so that we may speak.

In reading and hearing these words then, we become those who are entrusted with the words of God's promise. We who are called into being by these words are also those who are summoned to speak with these words. In this twofold sense, we are the community of the Word: created by the Word, entrusted with the word.

In and through these words we have said, God gives his Word, God commits himself to us and to the world. God does not promise himself to the church alone but to the world. The church is the people through whose words God gives his Word to the world.

Thus, in and through the words we speak here we speak to one another and to the world God's promise. As the community of the Word we are commissioned and authorized to promise God's reign of justice and mercy, God's coming to us and to our world, to deliver us from all forms of bondage. In our commission to bind and loose we are authorized to promise God's own saving work. In creation the earthling, as male and female, is commissioned to be the image and likeness of God—to represent God on the earth. In the commission to be the hearers and speakers of God's word of promise, we already begin to act as God's representatives, for in and through our words God gives his Word.

D. The Assurance of Faith

What does it mean to be the ones to whom these words are spoken? What does it mean to be those who are called into being by these words? What does it mean to be those to whom these words are entrusted? What does it mean to be the community in and through whose words God gives the divine Word (and so is committed) to the world?

We are the hearers and bearers of this assurance in and for the world. This assurance is certainly not for us alone. It is not the private possession of our community. It is meant for the world. Our question then is how we may so live in the world as to communicate this assurance.

Our world may often be seen to be one characterized by an open or secret despair. Certainly if violence is the symptom of despair then the sporadic and systematic violence that characterizes our world betrays an epidemic of despair. We despair of justice, we despair of reason, we despair of the other person and so we destroy the other person,

112

and we prepare to be destroyed by the other person ourselves. In short we despair. We are without hope for ourselves, for the other, for our world.

We distract ourselves from this despair. We busy ourselves with what we must know is unimportant. We become a society of endless consumption, of endless distraction. We fear silence and so bombard ourselves with messages and music, believing perhaps that if there is no silence we will not remember our despair. In the midst of this open and secret despair, we are commissioned to be bearers of hope, of assurance, of confidence.

The hope, assurance, and confidence we are commissioned to live out in the world is not to be confused with optimism. Optimism is the belief that things will get better, that there is a silver lining to the storm cloud on our horizon, that all will be for the best, that, as Micawber says, "Something will turn up." Optimism is superficial. It selects its evidence and extrapolates into the future. In this way it is like its cousin, pessimism. Both are superficial. Both extrapolate.

But the confidence of faith is more profound than either optimism or pessimism. It does not delude itself concerning the depth, the extent, or the intractability of human brokenness and bondage. It lives in and through the confession of sins, yet it does not give up on life. Its confidence is not in the world (things will work out) nor in itself (I can make it) but in God's word of promise. It is this that gives it the capacity to look at things as they are and not despair.

We who have been assured are to be the bearers of this assurance, this eschatological confidence, in and to our world. In order to be the sign of this confidence within the world, we must confront squarely the open and secret forms that   *113* despair and hopelessness take among us. I will suggest two ways we may live out this confidence, but I am sure many more will occur to you. The two ways of confidence are the way of steadfastness and the way of nonviolence.

1. The Way of Steadfastness

The words of assurance we repeat in our worship are words of promise. They assure us that God has not and will not give up on us. We live out the meaning of this assurance when we refuse to give up on ourselves, our neighbors, and our world. When despair grips our lives we became impatient with ourselves and one another. We give up on relationships and on commitments. We become frivolous in order to be fashionable. Our attention span is shortened. We begin many things, and finish few. We have little staying power. Our style of life conduces to this. We are interested in the newest or latest thing. We are mobile. Often we think of this as freedom, but it is really bondage, bondage to whim, to novelty, to false necessity. It is impatience born of despair. This becomes especially catastrophic when it also means that we become impatient with one another. Our friendships become fleeting and trivial. We are too ready to give up on friends, to acquire new ones and drop old ones. Even our marriages become scenes of impatience. The divorce rate is an index of this impatience, this secret despair.

The style of life formed by hope is quite different from all of this. Hope produces patience and patience produces steadfastness (Rom. 5:3-5). To live out the assurance of faith in a world of secret or open despair is to grow in steadfastness of purpose, in the capacity for loyalties that do not wither, commitments that endure. Because God does not give up on us we are less ready to give up on others. This is not because of blithe optimism. We know all too well how deep and intractable is the bondage and brokenness of our lives. We confess our sins, after all. We are not optimistic, but we are confident. We are confident that God comes to us and delivers us despite our bondage and brokenness.

And so we do not despair, of ourselves or of our neighbor. As God is faithful to us, so we live out this faithfulness in our steadfastness in commitments and in relationships. Since by God's promise we have been given time, we also have time for our neighbor. In our standing with the broken and bowed, the incurable and hopeless, the offensive and irritating, we demonstrate the assurance that God will stand by God's creation, that God will keep his word. Our steadfastness with people and with projects may be a sign of hope for the distracted, the impatient, and the despairing.

There are of course many dangers here. There is the danger we will give in to illusions about relationships, become merely stubborn in our projects. That is why the assurance we speak of here is always connected to the confession that exposes illusion and to the repentance that renounces willfulness. Steadfastness is not a new bondage. It is the fruit of hope, the embodiment of true freedom.

2. The Way of Nonviolence

The first covenant God made with us according to Genesis 9 was the promise not to destroy the earth and its inhabitants. In the life and death of Jesus, this covenant becomes flesh. The one who represents the reign of God suffers death at the hands of violence not in order to destroy, but to save.

In our world, now as then, violence is the 115

bloody hand of despair. It is the deed of hopelessness. If we see this clearly we will begin to seek ways to embody nonviolence in the midst of a violent world— not as an ideology to be mindlessly imposed on every situation, but as a witness to hope and confidence.

In the first centuries of Christian faith, this form of witness was self-evident.[4] It was regarded as inconceivable that one who was a Christian could also be a member of the military. After Constantine, as the church and state allied themselves to each other more closely, this contradiction was no longer so strongly felt. Today we have almost completely forgotten it, yet today it has become an urgent question as nations acquire the military capacity to destroy the earth. Despair has grown so great that we prepare ourselves to destroy all humanity in the name of national security. Nor is this capacity limited to the "superpowers." It is increasingly within the reach of nations large and small. What does it mean to be a witness to hope in the midst of this madness? What can it mean to turn from the "security" of despair to the confidence of hope?

There are those who claim that talk of nonviolence, of conscientious objection, of disarmament is unrealistic and utopian. They suppose that it is more realistic to engage in military expenditures that weaken or destroy the capacity of nations to build just societies or to meet the basic needs of their people. They suppose it is "realistic" to acquire the capacity to incinerate every man, woman, and child on the face of the earth in order to be more "secure." Perhaps they suppose, despite the overwhelming evidence of history, that we will never be

---

4. For a collection of early Christian documents on this issue, see Louis J. Swift, *The Early Fathers on War and Military Service* (Wilmington, Del.: Michael Glazier, 1983).

tempted to use weapons we have so carefully developed and deployed. Perhaps they suppose it is "realistic" to imagine that the widespread availability of weapons of mass destruction means they will never be used. This is not realism—it is sheer fantasy.

To live out the assurance of faith in the midst of a culture of despair is to counter that despair. One of the most urgent witnesses to hope in our day is the way of nonviolence, in our neighborhoods, in our nation, in our world. Whether this takes the form of conscientious objection, of restrictions on handguns, of opposition to capital punishment, of calls for disarmament, or some other form, the way of nonviolence is one of the ways open to us to be a sign of hope, a witness to the divine faithfulness, which is the ground of our hope.

We may find many other ways to live out the assurance of hope. In a world that so often appears to be governed by open and secret despair, the ways we choose to express our freedom will be beacons of hope. For us and for a despairing world, it is above all in the words of assurance addressed to us and entrusted to us that God gives his Word and so assures his world.

becomes a despairing cry and the words of assurance produce uncertainty and doubt. That all of this has actually happened to our worship makes clear how important it is that our liturgy more adequately express and enact its own meaning, aim, and foundation. Forgiveness must actually be pronounced or the whole of our worship is undermined.

Forgiveness may, of course, be announced and enacted in other ways than through the words of the formula for absolution. Indeed, the entire proclamation of the gospel in the Scripture and sermon may be, as Moltmann suggests, an expansion of the formula, "I absolve you."[1] This is as it should be. But it is by no means always true that the sermon does have this form and character. It may also take the form and character of an admonition or an exhortation, an edification, or God forbid, an accusation. So long as the sermon does not have the form and character of an announcement of God's promise and action, of the gospel of forgiveness and reconciliation, the sermon cannot take the place of the words of absolution.

The sacrament of the table (eucharist, mass, Lord's Supper, communion) is certainly a dramatic enactment of absolution, forgiveness, and reconciliation. In it the action and promise of God in Christ is dramatically acted out in a way to make mere words of absolution seem superfluous. Yet so long as our worship does not invariably have this eucharistic character it is not possible for us to speak of the superfluous character of absolution. It is essential that the declaration of forgiveness be expressed clearly and unambiguously in our service of worship.

---

1. Jürgen Moltmann, *The Church in the Power of the Spirit* (New York: Harper & Row, Publishers, 1977), p. 223.

In general then, we can say that where there is confession there must be absolution. This declaration of forgiveness can take many forms: the eucharist, the proclamation of the gospel, the formula of absolution. Regardless of its form, however, it must occur clearly and decisively and unmistakably if our liturgy is to reflect God's action in Christ and be the model for our life in the world on the basis of that action.

2. The Authority to Forgive

It is especially important to notice that we are commissioned here with the authority to forgive sins. How often people shy away from this authority, especially in "mainline" Protestant churches. Sometimes we seek to be more pious than God: "Only God can forgive sins," we say. Yet this is precisely the view contested by Jesus in the Gospels not only by his claim to this authority but through the commission and command he gives to his disciples. We are not only permitted to do this, we are actually commanded to do so.[2]

It has often been supposed that the regular role of religion (Christian or otherwise) is to teach people to be submissive, to impose on them patterns of belief and action that keep them in subservience to a priestly authority. The behavior of Jesus, which was regarded by the religious community of his day as blasphemous and irreligious, was to exercise authority over sin and sickness and to summon his disciples to exercise this same authority. This authority is focused in the words "your sins are forgiven."

---

2. See the discussion above in chapter 3.

The priesthood of believers recovered by the Reformation is clearly determined by a recollection of this commission. One of Luther's most fundamental principles was that the power to forgive sins was not restricted to a priestly elite but was the common right and responsibility of Christians.[3] It is a right and responsibility conferred not by ordination but by baptism. It was this principle that undermined the whole system of commercial indulgences and the corruption into which that system had plunged the Body of Christ.

This authority of the Christian is the opposite and enemy of any authoritarian system. It is an authority that sets the other free from the dominion of principalities and power, including those that take the form of authoritarian (and even "ecclesial") systems. Moreover, this authority is not the authority of those who are certain of their own "righteousness." It is the authority of the sinner. We who exercise this authority are those who know only too well our own brokenness, our own need for deliverance. Apart from this clarity and this yearning we have no authority.[4] Just as the sovereignty of Christ is the sovereignty of the crucified so our authority is the authority of those who participate in his death through our confession, repentance, and prayer for pardon.

But if what I have said concerning the priesthood of believers is true is there then any justification for the liturgical practice of putting these words in the mouth of the priest or pastor? This is a matter for the community itself to determine. The community as a

---

3. Luther, "Sacrament of Penance," p. 22. See also Bonhoeffer, *Life Together*, pp. 112-13.

4. This is the meaning of Bonhoeffer's assertion that "only the brother under the Cross can hear a confession," *Life Together*, p. 118.

whole must be responsible for the clarity of its witness, the appropriateness of its ritual performance.

Yet precisely because this is so it has normally seemed appropriate for the one who represents the community as a whole to be the one who speaks the words of absolution in the worship of the community. This is an appropriate reminder that the words are entrusted not to individuals privately but to the whole people of God. Unfortunately this policy has sometimes had the opposite effect. Instead of modeling the authority of the Christian in the worship of the community, the words of absolution have suggested the special authority of the priest or pastor. When this occurs we are not far from an authoritarian priesthood and a passive laity. The words, which are supposed to mobilize us, instead paralyze us.

Of course, there are other dangers that may accompany a different practice. If we are uncertain who is to speak these words the words themselves may be undermined with uncertainty. If it is left to the "inspiration of the moment" then we may again be led to forget that this authority is granted not by special experiences but by baptism. And if one without responsibility in and for the community speaks these words in the liturgy we may forget the necessary connection between responsibility and authority.

In general it seems to me to be best that one who represents the unity of the community should speak these words. But if this is done it becomes all the more crucial that this be understood as the action of the community as a whole, commissioned and commanded by its common Lord.

3. Words That Act

The assertion that you are forgiven or I absolve you is not simply a description of the   *123* way things are. This assertion actually intends to alter the way things are, to transform reality. The release and deliverance here announced is also performed and brought to pass.

We may find this strange at first. After all, words seem to us to be only ways of *naming* things. To use words to *change* things may seem like magic, part of a view of the world long since outmoded. When we attend more closely to our experience with language, however, we discover a variety of ways in which speaking alters rather than names the world.[5]

The most familiar example is to be found in the words we use to "get married." To say "I do" is to alter one's way of being in the world. These words are fateful, for they confer on two persons a new social, economic, and legal identity. The speaking of these words does not describe a situation but brings into being a new situation—it transforms a relationship into an institution.

Love and war are like each other not only in being situations in which we say "all's fair" but also in that both display the performative character of words. When war is "declared" a new situation comes into being—new laws and institutions emerge. Once again the situation is not merely described—it is fundamentally altered.

These are some of the most dramatic instances of the way some words have the power to alter the situation they refer to. There are many less dramatic examples. It is the common assumption of psychotherapy, for example, that carefully directed talking can not only

---

5. For an extended discussion of "performative utterance" see J. L. Austin, *How to Do Things with Words* (Oxford: Oxford University Press, 1962).

reveal but also alter the hidden dynamics of our action and way of being in relation to ourselves and our world. Hence we often call this kind of therapy "talk-therapy."

Speaking is not only an alternative to decisive action, it is also a way of acting. The Christian community is regularly reminded of this in its proclamation. Proclamation is the utterance of the Word of God. At first glance this seems quite preposterous. The words spoken here are, after all, only human words, our words. The one who speaks them is certainly not God but another human being like ourselves with similar doubts, brokenness, bondage. How then can this be God's Word?

In the preceding chapter we noticed that the Christian community is the community of the Word. We become this community by being addressed. This is done in our worship by the reading of Scripture, through which we are addressed by the earliest communities of faith. In being addressed by them, we are also addressed by God; through their words God gives us God's Word. But this in turn gives us words and summons us to speak with authority. This is accomplished in our worship by the sermon. In the sermon, one who represents the community as a whole speaks with authority, that is, in words authorized by the words of Scripture through which we are addressed. In and through the words of proclamation, God gives his Word. In this way the "preacher" proclaims "God's Word."

The proclamation is then an action. It is the action of the speaker through which God also acts. Paul speaks of the foolishness of preaching (I Cor. 1:17–2:5), which in its halting and all-too-human words is nevertheless that through which God saves the world. 125

This is precisely the way it is with the words of absolution or forgiveness. These are not "mere words" or "empty talk." They alter the situation, indeed they establish a new situation. In and through these words we are forgiven, we are released and absolved, for in and through these words God gives his Word, God commits himself to our deliverance and forgiveness. We who were godless and godforsaken are adopted, justified, forgiven, reconciled, and delivered.

4. The Repetition of Forgiveness

I have spoken of this absolution as the effective enactment of liberation, but if it is really effective what does it mean that it is repeated again and again in our liturgy? Why doesn't it seem to "take"?

We may even suppose that the very repetition of this action and of these words tends to deprive them of their power, their importance, their meaning. This is, I believe, a misunderstanding. Let us try a different illustration. A man and a woman meet. Over time they discover they love each other; at last one or the other of them actually gains the courage to say, "I love you." At length they are married. Every day one says to the other, "I love you." Are these words less meaningful after several months of repetition, after several years, after a lifetime of repetition?

We may not be sure. On the one hand they may have become "empty form." On the other they may have grown in meaning. The couple's years of experience with and knowledge of each other may increase the depth and breadth of their relationship and make possible this growth in meaning. So it is clear that the mere repetition does not empty the words of meaning. What does empty them of

126

meaning is if the words or actions here are said or performed unconsciously, without attention to them or investment in them. We may formulate it this way: If the words of love are spoken without love they become empty whether or not they are repeated. If the words of love are spoken with love they have meaning and grow in meaning with their repetition.

So also with the words of faith: Not through repetition but through unbelief are they emptied of their meaning. This is why in his treatise on penance (1519)[6] Martin Luther insisted on the centrality of faith. Without faith the words of forgiveness only do harm, immunizing us, as it were, from their effect. But in and with faith they strengthen and confirm us. He concludes, "Whoever believes, to him everything is helpful, nothing is harmful. Whoever does not believe, everything is harmful, nothing is helpful."[7]

Repeating these words then does not destroy their meaning. In fact it displays their meaning quite appropriately. In the first place, repeating the words of forgiveness distinguishes these words from the one and sufficient Word of God given in the life and ministry and destiny of Jesus of Nazareth. What we do in our liturgy is to represent the one action of God in Christ; our worship is not that action itself but a pointer to and indicator of that unique and unrepeatable action.

Beyond this the repetition of this liturgy makes clear that we are and remain those who need this forgiveness. Our deliverance is both fundamental and continual, already accomplished and still being accomplished. Indeed, because we know that the fundamental action of liberation has already been accomplished in Christ we have the hope that gives us the courage to

---

6. Luther, "Sacrament of Penance," p. 22.
7. Ibid.

continue to oppose and vanquish the powers of sin and death within and about us. Our repetition of this liturgy then is a reminder both of the one action already accomplished and of the continual and confident struggle made possible by that action. By the repetition of this liturgy, we gain greater clarity and lucidity about our situation.

Finally, in repeating these words and actions, we make clear that they are not an ephemeral and isolated feature of our life but the steady and growing pattern of our life. Just as in the words of love often repeated, so here as well: The very repetition makes clear that they express who we are, have been, and will be. They become the articulated rhythm of our life in the world.

The words of absolution or forgiveness then are repeated in our worship not because they are ineffective but so that they may have their true and proper effect.

B. The Life of Liberation

In our worship the forgiveness of sins is declared and demonstrated, but this is by no means the end of the matter. It is instead only the beginning, for in our worship we display the pattern of the life of faith. The forgiveness of sins in our daily lives in the world is the true meaning of this liturgy. But how are we to live out the meaning and reality of this declaration? It will mean that in a variety of ways our lives are to be an enactment of the liberation from bondage and brokenness, which we have declared to be accomplished in our service of worship.

1. Forgiving the Neighbor

128   Above all this must mean that we forgive the neighbor. And we begin here where it

seems most difficult—with the forgiveness of the ways our neighbor has wronged us. There is no alternative. We have already noticed (in chapter 3) that Jesus repeatedly stresses the importance of this forgiveness. Indeed, we regularly pray (whenever we pray the prayer Jesus taught his disciples), "Forgive us . . . *as* we forgive." We cannot participate in this liturgical action without making it the form and pattern of our life with our neighbor. Our forgiveness of the neighbor is the sign of the divine forgiveness we have declared in our worship.

What does it mean to forgive our neighbor? We all know the temptation to hold grudges, to nurse slights, to nurture in ourselves the sense that we have been wronged. Like a miser counting precious coins we keep an account of major and minor, real and imagined offenses. All of this produces a deep reservoir of bitterness, which, like an acid, eats away at us. It produces sickness of mind and body. Resentment corrodes the heart. It becomes itself a form of bondage and brokenness. Indeed it is one of the most terrible bondages. To forgive is to let go of this resentment. It is to let go of our grudges and slights. It is to bring out into the sunlight and fresh air the gnawed bones of our discontent. It is to be free.

And it is to free the neighbor. Forgiveness is not something that takes place only *within* us, it must also take place *between* us. Forgiveness does not mean leaving the other alone, leaving the situation unchanged. This is perhaps the most grievous and catastrophic misunderstanding of forgiveness. People often suppose that it means simply letting the other alone, that it refers to an attitude within us rather than an action that engages the neighbor. To forgive the other does not mean to suffer in silence. It means to act in a way that delivers the other from guilt, debt, and bondage.

We will not be able to do this without learning to see through the behavior of the other and the offense it gives us to the underlying bondage and brokenness of the other, which has given rise to the hurtful behavior. So long as we are preoccupied with our own hurt and resentment we will be unable to do this. But when we have begun to be freed of this resentment through confession and absolution, we may begin to see our neighbor as a cosufferer in bondage and brokenness. To the extent this happens we will be able to engage that bondage and brokenness with a healing and liberating word or deed. It is when we do this that we are truly engaging in the loosing, the absolving, the forgiving of the neighbor.

To forgive the neighbor then is not to leave the neighbor alone but to engage and encounter the neighbor. It is to encounter the neighbor with those deeds of love and liberation that release the neighbor from anxiety, from fear, from resentment, from guilt. Forgiveness is not passive, it is an aggressive assault on the dominion of sin in ourselves and in our neighbor.

It must not, however, become an assault on the neighbor. We all know the temptation to manipulate others, to coerce them into conforming with our wishes and desires, to make them over in our own image. This we must not do—for it is sin. It grows out of our own bondage to anxiety and seeks to bring the other into captivity to our desire. We must not do this violence to our neighbor, especially not in the name of setting the neighbor free. Our assault upon the dominion of sin, of anxiety, of fear and guilt must be quite circumspect. It must spring from a

130

fundamental commitment to the freedom of the other. We are granted dominion over sin. We are granted no dominion over our neighbor.

2. The Manifestation of Freedom

"The whole creation," writes Paul, "has been groaning in travail . . . [for] the glorious liberty of the children of God" (Rom. 8:22, 21). Like a woman in labor, the whole of creation groans in agony, desire, and hope. And what is the aim and goal of this yearning? It is the manifestation of freedom, of the freedom of that "leading edge" of the new creation, which we are.

With this language Paul places the disclosure of our freedom at the heart of the whole process and history of creation. Our freedom is not a private possession but is the point and aim of the travail of the earth itself. Thus our freedom must be manifest, apparent, on public display, and therefore not concealed or made a private matter. The freedom we enact in our liturgy belongs to the world and is given for the sake of the world.

But how is this freedom to be made manifest in and for the world? In the first place this occurs in and through our liturgy itself. The liturgy is the public performance and presentation of this liberty. In the liturgy we enact the drama of liberation within and for the sake of the world.

But this is by no means the end of the matter, for our liturgy shapes our life; it is the form and pattern of the life in Christ, which is to be embodied in and for the world. Thus our daily lives in the world including the public arena of politics and economics are to be a manifestation of freedom.

It is therefore important that we each consider those ways we can shape our style or manner of living in order to make of it a manifestation of freedom. Here the elements of unmasking illusion, of renouncing bondage, of solidarity with those who yearn for freedom, and of exhibiting confidence and steadfastness come together as a coherent pattern, which manifests freedom in the world. Beyond this we will need to ask if there are ways we can exhibit the freedom from anxiety and fear and guilt and self-preoccupation, which will confirm the presence of the freedom for which the whole earth yearns.

It is relatively easy to find dramatic examples of this freedom by attending to the life and witness of those who live this freedom in places of persecution and oppression: the singing in prison, the feasting of those who are threatened, the exhilaration of those who know the cost of discipleship. The story of the church in South Africa or South Korea or Poland demonstrates this freedom.

For those of us who live in less highly charged situations, it may seem more difficult to find ways of manifesting this freedom, yet it is both necessary and possible to do this. It is possible because every situation is one in which bondage and freedom oppose each other. It is necessary because our freedom is not our own possession but is a sign for the world that its agony is not in vain, that its destiny is freedom.

Our freedom is a sign. It is certainly not itself the final realization of the freedom for which we and all the earth hope. It is a foretaste, a preliminary indication, the "early returns." We know only too well that our freedom is incomplete, still struggling with both internal and external bondage. We also know that there will be no final liberation even for us until there is complete liberation for the world.

132   That is why it is important for us to be

heralds of this freedom and so a sign of hope for the world. Thus we exhibit in our lives that preliminary and partial freedom, which is the sign that we and all the earth will be set free.

3. Guardians of Liberty

We are called not only to exhibit freedom but to be its guardians. Paul writes to his congregations, You have been set free; do not yield your freedom (Gal. 5:1). Precisely because freedom is the sign of hope it is precious. It must be protected from that which would destroy it. "Eternal vigilance is the price of liberty"— Jefferson's watchword applies also here. But we also know all too well how often freedom is destroyed under the pretense of protecting it. We have witnessed this continually in our own political life as well as that of others. How can we be the guardians of freedom without being its executioners?

In the first place the liturgy itself is the public guardian of our liberty. In the liturgy we practice the vigilance that is the necessary companion of liberty. Here we wage the battle against the persistent erosion and subversion of freedom in our own hearts and lives. Without this practice in confession and repentance, in yearning and in assurance we would be defenseless against that within us and about us which would destroy our freedom. In performing this liturgy then we gain practice in exposing and renouncing bondage. This practice is our chief defense against the temptation to collaborate again in our own captivity. Here we learn how easy and how fatal it is to forfeit our freedom, to sell our inheritance for a bowl of pottage.

133

This action is the training of conscience. It is the sharpening and disciplining of a taste and sense for freedom, of the capacity to discriminate between freedom and bondage. But precisely as conscience begins to form, grow, and mature it is urgent that it not be compromised. Theology has long and consistently maintained that it is most dangerous to compromise our conscience for it is the presence in us of God's liberating Word. Of course many of us make trivial the idea of conscience—thinking of it as a kind of nagging superego. Often conscience has been spoken of in ways that seek to coerce people into conformity and compliance, but that is a travesty of conscience. The conscience is that which discriminates between freedom and bondage. It is the sign that freedom is taking form in us. Thus conscience must never be coerced nor may it be compromised. To destroy the conscience is to destroy the capacity for freedom.

Conscience must also not be confused with willfulness. Whim and willfulness are the most intimate forms of bondage. We cannot be free if we are subject to the most fleeting passions, the most capricious choices, the most arbitrary determinations of our hearts. Compared to this the most severe and constraining legalism is a kind of liberation. Conscience only grows where there is discernment and renouncing of bondage in our hearts and minds.

The freedom of conscience then is the most basic of all human rights, for in the presence and growth of conscience we see the nurture of freedom. This is one of the reasons Christians need to be champions of human rights both in their own land and in the world. Thus the defense of a person's freedom to worship, to have access to information (freedom of the press), to express his or her judgment (freedom of speech and assembly), and to be safeguarded against arbitrary penalties for practicing these rights (freedom from torture, arbitrary imprisonment, etc.) are essential to the growth of that conscience which is the sign of authentic freedom in the world.

If this is so then it means we must be guardians not only of our own conscience but of our neighbor's conscience as well. This is a theme Paul, the apostle of Christian liberty, repeats in several of his letters. Many of the Christians in the communities to which he writes had grown considerably in their understanding and experience of freedom, and Paul commended them for the strength of their freedom. But he also cautioned them to be careful that their freedom not become an offense to their weaker sisters and brothers (Rom. 14:1-23; I Cor. 8:1-13). The "stronger" knew that meat which had been offered to idols was not contaminated—they knew this because they knew that these idols had no power over those who had been set free. In this they were correct, so they thought it right to exhibit their freedom, but Paul warned them that others in the community might mistake this for participating in the worship of those idols. Their consciences would be offended. They might be led into doing what they believed to be wrong. This would destroy their conscience and so their freedom.

The exercise of our freedom must guard as well the conscience (and so the freedom) of the neighbor. This is an exceedingly fine line we must walk here, for we must compromise neither our own nor our neighbor's conscience. The clue to the proper procedure here is the language Paul uses of "weak" and "strong." We must not offend the weak, that is, lead them to do what they still believe to be wrong, but we are not to yield where weakness parades as strength. Much religious moralizing is the attempt   *135*

of those who know little of freedom (the weak) to
pretend to be the arbiters of freedom. In this pretense
they hedge in freedom and bind it about with law and
pretended "righteousness."[8] This must on no account
be permitted. We cannot yield an inch to this haughty
immaturity, this distorting and destroying of freedom.
This must be seen and named for what it is: weakness
rather than strength, immaturity rather than maturity.

But when this is done we must nevertheless guard
and nurture, not destroy or coerce the conscience of the
"weaker." We must so exhibit freedom that it respects
and nurtures the freedom of the neighbor. In this way
we will compromise neither our own freedom (which is
given and exhibited for the sake of the neighbor) nor the
freedom of the neighbor. In seeking to live this out in
our lives in the world, we will undoubtedly make many

---

8. The tendency of the "weak" to impose restrictions on the
"strong" was already recognized and vigorously contested in the
New Testament. The basis of this opposition is present in the
"woes" Jesus pronounces on the Scribes and Pharisees in the
twenty-fourth chapter of Matthew. The sum of his accusation
against them is that "they bind heavy burdens, hard to bear, and
lay them on men's shoulders; but they themselves will not move
them with their finger" (Matt. 23:4). This same polemic is the
basis of Paul's attacks on the "judaizers" in Galatians. Similarly,
after explaining the significance of the cross, the author of
Colossians concludes, "Therefore let no one pass judgment on
you in questions of food and drink or with regard to a festival or a
new moon or a sabbath. . . . Let no one disqualify you, insisting
on self-abasement and worship of angels, taking his stand on
visions, puffed up without reason by his sensuous mind" (2:16,
18). And in I Timothy we encounter a similar warning against
false teachers "who forbid marriage and enjoin abstinence
from foods which God created to be received with thanksgiving
by those who believe and know the truth" (4:3). These
repeated warnings should be understood as indicating a
fundamental principle of Christian ethics that distinguishes it from all forms of petty moralizing.

errors of judgment both on the one side and on the other, but precisely in and through the accompanying work of confession, repentance, and prayer for pardon we may grow in the capacity to be champions of freedom.

Is it necessary to add that we are learning how fragile and how precious is liberty in the world? Is it necessary now to emphasize that to champion liberty means also that we defend the freedom of the weak wherever it is threatened by those who pretend to be strong? Surely by now it is clear that the Christian must never compromise with tyranny—in religion, in economics, in politics. In these spheres freedom is the sign that the agony of the world is not in vain. We must not permit it to be snuffed out either by those who would openly destroy it or by those who would pretend to defend it. The church destroys itself when it sides against freedom in any sphere. Even worse, it transforms the gospel of liberation into a sanction for oppression. In its life the church has to its shame given credibility to Marx's assertion that "religion is the opium of the people," which makes them content with their chains. We cannot defend freedom if we do not confess and renounce our complicity in bondage.

4. Agents of Liberation

We are not only those who have been set free and so manifest and defend freedom. We are also those who are commissioned to absolve, to set at liberty, to be agents of liberation. Every Christian has this authority and this responsibility. This commission does not stop at the frontier of the interpersonal. It carries us into the sphere of the public life in the world of society, of politics, and of economics. If we do not penetrate these spheres with the deeds   *137* of liberation then the world is left without a witness to the liberating intention and action of God in Christ.

It is important therefore that we find ways to engage those spheres of life as agents of liberation. This will mean that we see clearly the systemic structures of death and bondage and that we respond to these forcefully and imaginatively. It is inappropriate at this point to provide an economic or political program Christians must follow. The freedom of the Christian must be respected and nurtured, not coerced. We may find ourselves engaged with these structures in quite different ways. We have different gifts, different tasks, different spheres of influence, different opportunities and responsibilities. This diversity is one of the most characteristic features of our common life. To become a Christian does not mean to put on a uniform, to uphold a party line, to march in lockstep. It means to become responsible agents of freedom.

The diversity of the Christian life-style is itself a sign of freedom and as such it must be preserved, but this diversity springs from a common liberation and aims at the freedom of the earth. Thus the diversity is not a mere collection of disparate ways of life. It has a common base, a common theme, a common goal. Accordingly, when the opportunity arises Christians will find ways to oppose economic exploitation, cultural imperialism, and political oppression. These have long been self-evident as principles of action and commitment for most of the major organizations of Christians. What has all too often been lacking is the translation of these commitments into concrete action in particular circumstances.

But what sort of liberating action are we to perform? Certainly if we have begun to glimpse the immensity of human suffering,

138

brokenness, and bondage in our world we may feel there is little or nothing we can do to affect the condition of our neighbor. It may be that this sense of the overwhelmingness of the problem creates some of our passivity when confronted with social injustice. There is no question that the problems are immense, but this by no means need produce despair or complacency. Ours is not the impossible task of accomplishing liberation. Ours is the mission of bearing witness to the liberation which is already being accomplished by God in Christ through the Spirit.

We have already seen how in and through our words God gives the divine Word. This is true as well for our deeds of liberation in all the spheres of our lives in the world. God is at work in his world to save and deliver, to heal and to liberate. Through our deeds of liberation the action of God becomes visible in the world. When we act on behalf of the prisoner, the poor, the oppressed, then the promised deliverance of God becomes visible in the world. "If it is by the finger of God that I cast out demons, then the kingdom of God has come upon you," said Jesus in the Gospel of Luke (Luke 11:20). His activity of healing, of exorcizing, of feeding the hungry, of befriending the outcast were all signs that the reign of God was at hand, that God gave and kept the divine Word. Jesus was himself this Word in person, and he commissions his disciples to be those who continue in that mission and ministry.

When we, either directly or through our representatives, heal the sick; feed the hungry; overthrow oppression; establish justice; bring peace; and oppose exploitation, racism, militarism, and imperialism, then through our action the promise and action of God becomes visible in the world. We do not do this on our own. God will be true to the divine Word whether we act or not, but through   *139* our action God's action becomes visible as a sign of hope, and an assurance of liberation for the earth.

To engage in deeds of liberation then is not to seek to remake the world or to "bring in the kingdom of God." It is to witness to the remaking of the world already begun in Jesus, to the reign of God, which has already drawn near in him. This is why our action is so important. For no area of life must be left without a witness to the coming reign of the one who will be "all in all." Where there is no witness there is no hope. And where there is no hope our world plunges all the more swiftly into chaos, into tyranny, into despair. The world must know that God is pledged to its deliverance and to the abolition of every form of bondage. However "ineffective" our political action, it is the sign of this promise, the making visible of this action, and so a summons to hope.

Conclusion

In the course of these reflections on the confession and forgiveness of sins, I have suggested a number of ways the actions we perform in our worship may become the pattern of our lives in the world. There are a great many ways we may expose illusion, renounce our own complicity in the structure of bondage, exhibit solidarity with those who yearn for liberation, become signs of assurance and agents of liberation. Indeed, you may feel that far too much has been proposed, too many options, too much to do. If so, then at the close of these reflections on the liturgy it is appropriate to recall the words of Jesus: "Do not be anxious" (Matt. 6:25, 34).

Above all the style of life that reflects the pattern of our worship is one that exhibits freedom, is grounded in freedom, provokes freedom. By its nature freedom cannot be reduced to a recipe or a program. The life formed by this liturgy of liberation is not an anxious adherence to a series of obligations and regulations. Each of our life-styles will be characterized by distinctive emphases, different rhythms, alternative ways of bringing freedom to expression. In the liturgy we join together cheerfully and confidently to enact the freedom for which Christ has set us free and to enable one another to exhibit this freedom more clearly and decisively in our lives in the world. As this liturgy shapes our style of life more and more, we gain practice in the display of joyful and confident freedom.

We who participate in the liturgy of liberation become signs of hope in and for the world. In the *ekklesia* we gather to take action for the deliverance of the world. Our action reflects the action of God in Christ and forms our life in the world. In our life in the world, in our manner and style of life, we become the visible sign of the promised reign of God.

PART THREE

Implications

The Practice of Confession in the Community of Faith

10

I n the preceding chapters we have examined the liturgy of liberation, attending particularly to the way it can shape our lives in the world. In these last three chapters I will draw some conclusions from the preceding discussion for the life of the church itself. Thus, having attended to some of the ways our action within the community of faith shapes our lives in the world, we turn now to reconsider the internal life of the community in order to discover ways a renewed appreciation of the liturgy may affect that life. In chapter 11, I will suggest ways the liturgy of liberation may serve as the form or structure of pastoral care and counseling, and in chapter 12 I will propose a reconsideration of the sacramental character of this liturgy. Thus, in those chapters we will attend to what our discussion implies for professional practice (the ministry of pastoral care) and for sacramental and ecumenical theology.

Before turning to these specific topics, however, it is important to see how the activity of the confession and forgiveness of sins may become a more vital part of the life of the community of faith as a whole. Thus this chapter will summarize some of the results of our discussion of the liturgy of liberation and draw some conclusions for the life and practice of the worshiping community.

A. The Liturgy of the Congregation

In the liturgy of the *ekklesia*, we confess our sins, repent of them, pray for pardon, hear and

144

speak words of assurance and absolution. The meaning of these elements depends, as we have seen, on their aim and goal—the forgiveness of sins. It is in this action that we affirm our faith; it is this action that we are commissioned and commanded to perform by Jesus. The other actions prepare for and so amplify this central and fundamental action. The enactment and pronouncement of liberation itself is the basis of all that we do in this liturgy of liberation.

Because this is so, the action we perform here in the worship of the community points to and represents the action of God in Christ. Our liturgical action does not stand on its own but is a replica or model of the action of God through Christ. In him God has come to us in mercy. God turned toward us when we were turned away from God. God has come to us to deliver us from our self-chosen bondage and brokenness. Paralyzed by fear, anxiety, guilt, and self-preoccupation, we have been mobilized by God's word and act of deliverance.

Our action in the liturgy is not a mere reminder of this action of God. It is rather the case that in and through our words God gives God's own Word; that in and through our actions, God's action is made manifest. We are commissioned, commanded, and authorized to loose our neighbors from the power of sin and bondage. We are assured that in our forgiveness, God forgives; in our absolution, God absolves; in our liberating, God liberates. We do not confuse our action with God's action. Our action remains a human action. But through this human action, which by itself is ineffective, God acts in an effective way "to set at liberty those who are oppressed."

Our action in the liturgy is not an action separated from the rest of our lives in the world. The liturgy itself is a public dem-   145 onstration in and for the world of God's liberating action and intention. But it is also the form and pattern of Christian existence in and for the world. The action of the people (liturgy) forms the life of the people of God in the world. The enactment of the liturgy of liberation creates a liberating praxis. In the confession of sins, we learn to penetrate and expose the internal and external illusions that hold us captive. In repenting of sins we learn to renounce the seductions of bondage and oppression. In the prayer for pardon, we practice solidarity with those who yearn for justice and righteousness. In the hearing and speaking of assurance and absolution, we become practiced in the deeds of liberation, which manifest the freedom God intends for his world.

The liturgy of liberation then serves to demonstrate the action of God and to model our action in and for the world. It is therefore not a dispensable, but an essential, part of our worship and of our life. It is quite clear that for many of our congregations the liturgy has lost this place of importance and has fallen into disuse or has become simply routine. Insofar as this has happened we have lost this essential practice in and dramatization of the authority and responsibility of Christian existence. We no longer know what it means to rely on (believe in) "the forgiveness of sins." This can only be remedied by permitting this liturgy to again emerge as a prominent action of the community of faith—of our life together.

It has been one of my principal theses that what we do in our public worship shapes our perception and our action. If our public worship is misshapen it will distort our understanding of ourselves in relation to both God and the world, and it will distort our ways of acting in these relationships. Our worship then becomes the false and demonic worship against which the prophets (and also Jesus and Paul and John) protested. In another book I have shown how this is true of our public performance of prayer and praise.[1] It is no less true of our public performance of the liturgy of liberation.

The most urgent question here has to do with the enactment and pronouncement of forgiveness or absolution. I have already argued that this is the indispensable aim and goal of the acts of confession and repentance. Without the clear presence of this word of forgiveness, our confession becomes moralistic or obsessive, our repentance becomes an empty gesture or a nihilistic refusal of self and world, our prayer for pardon is unanswered or uncertain, our words of assurance undermine rather than establish our faith. The declaration of pardon, forgiveness, and absolution is that which makes possible our confession, repentance, and prayer for pardon (chapters 4 and 9).

Beyond this I have argued that we are clearly and expressly authorized, commissioned, and commanded to speak this word (chapter 3). It is of the essence of our vocation as Christians that we act in the name of God to forgive sin.

But what form is this pronouncement and enactment to take? It may take the form of a first-person declaration like that of the traditional formula for the sacrament of penance (*ego te absolvo*: I absolve you). It may take the form of Jesus' declaration to the paralytic, "Your sins are forgiven." It may take the form of the assurance of Paul, "[Nothing can] separate us from the love of God in Christ Jesus" or of I John, "Your sins are forgiven for his sake." What is crucial, I believe, is that there be a clear pronouncement. It should not be

---

1. Theodore W. Jennings, Jr., *Life as Worship: Prayer and Praise in Jesus' Name* (Grand Rapids: Wm. B. Eerdmans Publishing Co., 1982), pp. 62-80, 110-24.

"conditional" (if you repent . . .) for it represents the unconditional love of God, which justifies the ungodly. Besides, all the conditions that might be offered here are already present in the liturgy itself. The conditional phrase (if we confess, if we repent, if we seek pardon) has its appropriate place at the beginning of the sequence as the call to confession. To substitute a conditional clause for the pronouncement of forgiveness is to take away the clarity and confidence, which make the confession and repentance possible as acts of freedom and joy.

The unconditional declaration of forgiveness is by no means alien to the traditions of Protestant worship. In his revision of the form of the mass, Luther speaks of the pronouncement of "the Peace of the Lord" as "a public absolution of the sins of the communicants, truly the Gospel voice announcing remission of sins, the one and most worthy preparation for the Lord's table, if it be apprehended by faith and not otherwise than as though it came forth from the mouth of Christ Himself."[2] Similarly, in the development of a reformed liturgy in Strassburg by Martin Bucer, the words of assurance (I Tim. 1:15; John 3:16; Acts 10:43; or I John 2:1-2) are followed by: "Thus, in His [Christ's] name I proclaim unto you the forgiveness of all your sins and declare you to be loosed of them on earth, that you be loosed of them also in heaven, in eternity. Amen."[3] A much longer form of declaration is proposed by Calvin in his account of the form of worship in use in his community in Basle.[4]

It is of course true that the declaration of pardon and

---

2. *Liturgies of the Western Church,* selected and introduced by Bard Thompson (Philadelphia: Fortress Press, 1961), p. 112.

3. Ibid., p. 170.

148   4. Ibid., p. 214.

absolution is by no means the universal practice of Protestant churches. In some cases (the liturgy of John Knox or that of the English puritans), the prayer of confession, repentance, and pardon is followed immediately by the sermon, which is intended to announce and explain the gospel and so serves in the place of an absolution. This practice, to the extent to which the sermon had not only the place but also the form and content of an announcement of forgiveness and freedom, corresponds to Moltmann's assertion that the form of every sermon is or ought to be: "*Ego te absolvo*," I release you.[5]

By now it should be evident that I believe it is essential that the declaration of forgiveness, pardon, absolution, or liberation be clearly expressed as the culmination of any sequence of confession, repentance, and prayer for pardon. Only in this way will our worship adequately reflect its basis in the act of God in Christ and the commission to engage in the forgiveness of sins, which Christ confers on the community of faith.

Beyond this there is considerable scope for variation and adaptation. In any variation it is important that what we do and say be as clear as possible. Our confession must not be evasive or our repentance half-hearted. The more concrete and vigorous our language here the better will be conveyed the liberating action, which is the theme of this liturgy.

B. Inner Appropriation

Some may object to this attention to the form of our worship by insisting on the greater importance of the faith, which is enacted in the worship. Is not all this talk of liturgy a preoccupation with mere

---

5. Moltmann, *Church in the Power of the Spirit*, p. 223.

forms and externals? Is not the way we live and the faith by which we live far more important than the form of our public worship? Throughout I have insisted that this "form" actually shapes both faith and life and so cannot be disconnected from them. Yet it is also the case that the most carefully constructed liturgy is worthless if it is not appropriated by faith for faith.

Thus it is important to speak of the inner appropriation of these actions. Their proper public demonstration is certainly not an end in itself. Without serious and intentional engagement these actions become an empty and vain repetition. This is why Luther speaks of the importance of faith, which invests itself in and relies on these actions.

The ritual action we perform together makes us practiced in the works of confession and repentance. It is as we do these things here in the congregation that we learn to do them "for ourselves." Thus these actions serve as a pattern for our reflection on our lives in the world. This thoughtful inner appropriation of the liturgy enables us to live more consciously, intentionally, and intelligently. We need not undertake this reflection and appropriation in a particularly pious way. It is simply the pattern of a life that seeks critical clarity concerning itself in order to live more humanely and freely.

This activity of inner appropriation makes it possible to engage all the more fruitfully in the liturgy of the gathered community, just as participating in that liturgy provides us with a pattern for the intelligent self-assessment of an inner appropriation. Thus the public liturgy and the private reflection belong with each other and complement each other.

The chief danger of self-assessment is that it may lead to self-preoccupation, to an obsessive policing of our own lives, motives, relationships. This danger arises precisely because we cannot

150

"forgive ourselves." Forgiveness, liberation, and deliverance come necessarily from another person.[6] I cannot say to myself, "Your sins are forgiven" or "I absolve you." For this word to be spoken it must invade my solitude, it must be addressed to me by another. Here as in other areas of our lives we are reminded of the fundamental structure of our existence—that we need another in order to be fully human. Our life, as a human life, is composed of relationships. Neither love nor freedom is possible for us alone.

Thus the self-assessment we may engage in cannot be complete without the aid or help of another. This is why meditation requires liturgy, faith requires community.

Even with both liturgical order and its personal appropriation, we may still sense that these remain somehow "abstract." We may still wish for a more penetrating and clarifying process of confession, repentance, and absolution in our life in the community. There are at least two ways such a process has been embodied in the life of the community apart from the formal liturgy. They are the practice of "private confession" and he forming of small groups for the purpose of mutual confession.

C. Private Confession

Apart from the liturgy itself the most characteristic form of Christian nurture in Western Christendom has been the private confessional understood as the sacrament of penance. In Protestant traditions the sacrament of penance has been largely replaced by various forms of pastoral care and counseling performed by ordained clergy. While there may be good reason to assign certain tasks to those who by virtue of training and ordination are

---

6. See Bonhoeffer, *Life Together*, pp. 115-16.

qualified for special responsibility, this must never be permitted to become a substitute for the responsibility of the whole people of God. Each Christian is summoned into the priesthood of all believers to represent and enact the liberating action of God in Christ. Some elements of the practice of the private confessional may help us to prepare less formal patterns of mutual aid in the work of forming a life more reflective of the gospel.

The procedure may be relatively informal and quite flexible. Either for the purpose of dealing with a particular situation or for the purpose of a long-term project of growth and change I may enlist another person whose wisdom and discernment I trust, whom I trust to be my "confessor," guide, or spiritual director. It may only be for an evening or this relationship may last for several years. The "confessor" or guide may be a close friend or someone I know only by reputation. And what do I ask of such a guide? I ask that she or he help me to see more clearly the forces and structures that distort my life. I ask for encouragement in resolutely renouncing those forms of bondage and brokenness of which I become aware. I ask that he or she join with me in turning toward freedom and wholeness, strengthen me with words of assurance, and pronounce forgiveness. In short I ask this person to "speak the truth in love" (Eph. 4:15 NEB). But you may ask, Isn't that what friends are for? Exactly. We all need this aid and comfort. We are all called to give this aid and comfort.

One of the features of the traditional confessional was the assignment of particular works of satisfaction. The instinct here was a sound one, but the tendency to focus on specifically "religious" acts was, I believe, a fundamental distortion. What is important is that this process facilitate the formation of a life-style that exhibits the marks of freedom we have discussed in the preceding chapters. Forming

152

life, not performing special works of satisfaction, is what is important here. Luther had a sure instinct when in this connection he spoke of the importance of love rather than prayers and candles.[7] But even more important, Luther saw that forgiveness does not depend on the "works" of satisfaction, but instead that it is the forgiveness or liberation that produces an altered life. No legalistic prescription can produce freedom, but growth in freedom must be the aim of the practice of confession. Thus it is appropriate that the focus here be not on works that satisfy a law but on a life that exhibits more clearly the freedom for which Christ has set us free.

Perhaps the best-known advocate of the renewed and reformed practice of private confession among modern Protestant theologians is Dietrich Bonhoeffer.[8] In his *Life Together* he maintains that this practice of confession opens upon the way to community, to the cross, to certainty. It is the way to community since it abolishes the masks and illusions that separate us from one another. It is the way to the cross because it entails renouncing the old world and self and turning toward the new. It is the way to certainty because the word of forgiveness is made concrete in the voice of the brother or sister.

---

7. Luther, "Sacrament of Penance," p. 21.
8. Not only here but throughout this entire discussion of the confession and forgiveness of sins my reflections have been provoked and guided by Bonhoeffer's *Life Together*. Indeed that book more than any other has provided the impetus for me to embark on a "theology of the church," which began with *Life as Worship*. In connection with confession and forgiveness, it seems to me that Bonhoeffer's view remains too "individual" and private, but I believe that the opening toward social and political reality is implicit in Bonhoeffer's later work *Ethics* and his *Letters and Papers from Prison*.   153

In an age of intense specialization, we may be unsure of our capacity to engage in this sort of help for one another. We are all too inclined to substitute professional services for this neighborly aid and assistance. There are undoubtedly times when we need the special services of persons trained in psychology and psychiatry, but all Christians are authorized and commanded to engage in the work of the forgiveness of sin. The surrender of this authority and responsibility to a priestly or professional class is the death of Christian freedom.

D. Group Confession

A further possibility for the practice of confession is the small group that gathers for the purpose of mutual examination, exhortation, and encouragement. The model for this was devised by Wesley as the basic organizational unit of the societies he founded. In our own day the small group and house church movements have sprung up making use of a variety of methods taken over from third force or humanistic psychology. Although we may feel that the Wesleyan groups were too legalistic and narrowly "pious" and that the "encounter" or "house church" groups tend to become too "faddish" or too far separated from the gospel, we may nevertheless see in these group settings a further effort to express more concretely the essential practice of confession and liberation.

Perhaps the most ambitious attempt to make use of the small group for purposes of confession and encouragement was that launched by John Wesley to "conserve the fruits of the revival" of which he was the leader in eighteenth-century England. The "class meetings" served as the basic unit of Wesley's "societies." All members of the society were also expected to be a part of such a class, which would meet weekly for the purpose of mutually examining the temptation, sin, and progress toward sanctification of each of its members.[9] As so often happens such classes could become the occasion of considerable hypocrisy and "spiritual pride,"[10] but there is also no denying their great power and influence in the forming of Christian life in eighteenth-century and early nineteenth-century English Methodism.

Is it possible to adapt elements from this Wesleyan experiment for the purpose of a more concrete expression and experience of the liturgy of liberation? It would be necessary to guard against those tendencies that subvert the proper aim of such a group, which is to liberate one another from bondage. Substituting a religious bondage for a "worldly" bondage is no great bargain. It would be crucial to keep attention focused on the "nonreligious" dimensions of bondage and brokenness to which we have referred in these pages.

---

9. The rules that govern these societies may be found in *The Works of John Wesley*, ed. Thomas Jackson, v. VIII (3rd ed. 1872, reprinted 1979) (Grand Rapids, Mich.: Baker Book House Co.), pp. 269-74. In his "Plain Account of the People Called Methodists," Wesley affirms that what is fundamental to these societies is "the confession of several persons conjointly, not to a priest, but to each other" (ibid., p. 259).

10. Wesley himself recognized this danger and fought strenuously against it. "The thing which I was greatly afraid of all this time was, a narrowness of spirit, a party zeal, a being straitened in our own bowels, that miserable bigotry which makes many unready to believe that there is any work of God but among themselves" (ibid., p. 257).

But with these qualifications it may very well be that gathering regularly in informal groups to assist one another in gaining clarity about our situation in the world, and in gaining courage to form styles of life expressive of freedom in a world dominated by bondage, could help greatly in the formation of freedom.

In Latin American Christianity, the rapidly growing movement of "base communities" is an especially striking illustration of the effectiveness of group "confession" in the form of a diagnosis of the structures and forces that prevent genuine freedom and dignity. These base communities are communities of the poor who meet together for prayer and Bible study and for the purpose of engaging with the gospel the socioeconomic and political forces that enforce their poverty and disenfranchisement. Confession then is a movement of "conscientization," which brings into sharp relief the ways in which life is disfigured by structures of oppression and by the sense of powerlessness such structures encourage.[11] Thus repentance may take the form of a renunciation of powerlessness and fear, of a sense of futility and resignation, in favor of a spirited turning toward concrete acts of solidarity and liberation. Our discussion in preceding chapters of the socioeconomic interpretation of sin as bondage and of forgiveness as liberation makes clear that the growth of such base communities represents not only a legitimate but also an essential dimension of the witness of faith. For Christian faith, if it is to be faithful to Christ, must give public testimony to the way in which the principalities and powers are overcome in his death and resurrection.

North America has also seen a renewed appreciation for

---

11. Abundant literature is now available on the generating of a liberation theology from the shared and reflected experience of such base communities. Among the most

the role of small groups of Christians who seek to examine their lives in the light of hope for release from brokenness and bondage. One such group is the "house church" movement, which seeks to appropriate some of the tools of humanistic or third force psychology to deal more adequately with individual and interpersonal forms of brokenness and bondage.[12] Confession then takes the form of becoming clear about the ways events and relationships in the past continue to paralyze one in the present. Repentance may then take the form of confronting feelings long suppressed, of renouncing destructive patterns of intrapersonal and interpersonal relationships.

By itself the emphasis on conscientization directs attention to the external sources of bondage and one's complicity in them. In contrast the house church movement focuses on the internal and interpersonal sources of bondage and brokenness. Both illustrate ways in which small groups of Christians may participate in the diagnosis and renunciation of bondage and in the turn toward and enactment of freedom. Perhaps the most important role of the Wesleyan class meetings, the Latin American base communities, and the North American house churches is that they clearly exhibit the authority of the "laity," of the whole people of God, to engage in the

interesting are Hugo Assmann, *Theology for a Nomad Church* (Maryknoll, N.Y.: Orbis Books, 1976); José Miguez Bonino, *Doing Theology in a Revolutionary Situation* (Philadelphia: Fortress Press, 1975); and Juan Luis Segundo, *The Liberation of Theology* (Maryknoll, N.Y.: Orbis Books, 1976). Against those who argue that all of this is "only" political, Gustavo Gutierrez demonstrates the profound spiritual journey that is entailed in any process of liberation in *We Drink from Our Own Wells: The Spiritual Journey of a People* (Maryknoll, N.Y.: Orbis Books, 1984).

12. For a discussion of the form of "house church," which makes use of the tools of humanistic psychology, see *Chicago Theological Seminary Register*, December 1970, February 1973, and November 1973.

work of liberation. Moreover they attest to the power of a community of equals to assist one another in the mutual task of becoming more and more clearly the signs of freedom and responsibility within the world. What is crucial for the groups we may find ourselves in is that we remember that the basis for what we do together is the messianic action of Christ and that the confrontation with sin is not to be restricted to moral or psychological or political categories, but is to engage the entirety of our lives as these are claimed by Christ and transformed into a new creation.

Conclusion

"Confession is not a law, it is an offer of divine help for the sinner." So wrote Bonhoeffer in his *Life Together*.[13] For many of us most of the time, the liturgical performance and conscientious inner appropriation of the liturgical action will seem an adequate assistance in growing into the life of freedom. Others will wish to experience this liturgy more concretely in the form of private or group confession and absolution. There is no law here, only the opening of possibilities for the life of freedom in the world. Whether in formal liturgy or private meditation, in personal or group practice in confession, it is crucial that we not lose sight of the goal. For what we seek is not to become more and more separated from the world in the larger or smaller ghettos of religious practice, but to become more faithful witnesses in the world to that liberty God promises to the whole creation. The practice of confession must not become a way of withdrawal from the world but a preparation for engagement in the world—for the sake of the world—on the basis of the gospel.

13. P. 117.

Confession and Pastoral Care

11

D iscussing the meaning of the liturgy of confession and forgiveness and its application to life in the world and in the church would be incomplete without some attention to the pastoral practice that has arisen out of the tradition of the confessional. Accordingly, in this chapter I will mention some of the general implications for the practice of pastoral care and counseling that follow from the perspective on the liturgy of liberation advanced in preceding chapters. The aim is not to provide a definite program for the theology of pastoral care but to offer avenues of dialogue between the theological perspective I have proposed and the practice of pastoral care.

A. Pastoral Care and Pastoral Liturgy

The emergence of the "pastoral care" movement in North American Protestantism has profoundly affected the institutional life of seminaries, churches, and hospitals, and has generated its own institutions, journals, and professional organizations.[1] This move-

---

1. For the definitive history of pastoral care and counseling in the United States, see E. Brooks Holifield, *A History of Pastoral Care in America* (Nashville: Abingdon Press, 1983).

ment has been characterized by the appropriation of insight, theory, and therapeutic technique from the burgeoning fields of psychology, psychoanalysis, and psychotherapy. The turn toward psychology, which characterizes the emergence of a relatively affluent society following the Second World War, has succeeded in becoming more or less self-evident as a stable feature of cultural and ecclesial life. The pastoral care movement is the carrier and expression of this revolution of consciousness in the church.

Despite certain caveats, which may be introduced concerning the historical and socioeconomic conditions to which the emergence and the success of this movement may be attributed, there is no denying the importance of its contribution to the reshaping of ministerial practice in order to meet real and urgent human need. The appropriation of a host of theoretical and therapeutic perspectives from the domain of psychology has enabled contemporary Christianity to respond creatively and imaginatively to an entire range of human affliction. This extension of the church's healing ministry is one of the most important developments in its life of the last several decades.

Yet the very rapidity of the emergence and profusion of theoretical and therapeutic models has often resulted in a crisis of identity for practitioners of pastoral care. Put briefly, this crisis takes the form of uncertainty regarding the pastoral, ecclesial, or theological identity of the care and counseling that is offered on the basis of psychological insight. After the initial excitement of novel insight begins to fade and the pastoral counselor finds himself or herself collaborating closely and perhaps competing with persons fully expert in psychological theory and practice, the question of a specifically pastoral identity obtrudes with growing urgency.[2]

I believe that the specifically *pastoral* identity of pastoral counseling may be seen best if we view it as rooted in the primary responsibilities of ministry. Whether or not the practitioners of pastoral care are ordained, the care and counsel they offer should be viewed as an expression and application of the central liturgical ministries of "word and sacrament." To the extent to which pastoral care, counseling, or psychotherapy are viewed in this way, avenues will be opened for recovering a clear sense of pastoral identity, without forfeiting the analytical and therapeutic insights of modern psychology. Clarifying the pastoral character of pastoral care then depends on the possibility of understanding pastoral counseling as an extension of the liturgical leadership fundamental to the definition of Christian ministry.

There are many ways this task may be prosecuted, as many as there are liturgical actions that serve as paradigms for pastoral practice. For our purposes, however, the series of actions I have called the liturgy of liberation have central significance. Indeed modern pastoral care may be understood as the continuing and transforming of traditional Christianity's practice of the confessional. This practice has often been understood as a distinct sacramental action and as an indispensable preparation for participating in the sacramental worship of the community.

---

2. For two different but equally provocative treatments of the theme of pastoral identity in pastoral care, see Paul W. Pruyser, *The Minister as Diagnostician* (Philadelphia: Westminster Press, 1976) and Thomas C. Oden, *Pastoral Theology* (San Francisco: Harper & Row, Publishers, 1983).

Many practitioners of pastoral care may be alarmed by an attempt to view pastoral counseling as the heir of this long and rich ecclesial tradition. The confessional has sometimes been associated with judgmental moralism or with a preoccupation with superficial symptoms. But the discussion of confession, repentance, and forgiveness supplied by earlier chapters (and to be applied here) should serve to allay these fears.

In pastoral care and counseling we are concerned with the liberation of persons from bondage to the distorted dynamics of desire and anxiety, and with the healing of the brokenness occasioned by this bondage. The liturgical paradigm for deliverance from bondage and brokenness is provided by the sequence: call to confession, confession, repentance, prayer for pardon, assurance, and absolution. Viewing pastoral care as the exemplification and application of this liturgical model in the realm of prolonged and disciplined hearing and speaking will not only emphasize the pastoral identity of this counseling and therapeutic practice but may also suggest to pastoral counselors some new ways to evaluate and shape their own theory and practice.

B. The Call to Confession

Establishing a pastoral counseling relationship entails the assurance of acceptance and confidentiality together with the offer of concrete assistance in the project of healing, liberation, and growth. These characteristics correspond to the liturgical and sacramental practice of confession and so to the invitation to confession, which is the opening element of the liturgical practice of confession.

Apart from the absolute assurance of confidentiality, no pastoral relationship is possible. In this lies one of the distinctive advantages of the *pastoral* counselor as opposed to the medical or purely psychological one. There is a long tradition of absolute confidentiality in the practice of the confessional that assures the one who comes to a pastor or priest that the latter's lips are "sealed" not only by individual inclination and historical custom but by an ecclesial law that secular law is bound to acknowledge. Even in the practice of group confession found in Wesley's "select societies," the rule "What is spoken here is never spoken again"[3] was strictly enforced. Already, with this tradition of the "seal of the confessional," pastoral care asserts its specifically ecclesial identity.

The call to confession in the liturgy of the church contains the assurance that those who confess their sins will in no way be rejected or abandoned. The saying of John 6:37, that the one who comes to me I will not cast out, could well be the motto on the door of every pastoral counselor. The crucial aspect in the discipline of pastoral care and counseling is the building of an accepting attitude and style, which actively gives permission to those who come for help to disclose themselves fully and freely. This disclosure is only possible where there is full assurance that there will be no "judgmental" or rejecting response on the part of the pastor. In building a relationship of trust based on nonjudgmental acceptance, the pastoral counselor heeds the evangelical command of Jesus: "Judge not." Taking this injunction with full seriousness is one of the marks of a disciplined pastoral care that sets it apart from the pastoral "malpractice" of condemnatory attitudes and responses formerly character-

---

3. *Works of John Wesley* (1872) vol. VIII, p. 261.

istic of many untrained pastors. The establishing of ways of training persons in nonjudgmental and accepting styles must be counted one of the most important achievements of clinical pastoral education. This discipline does not simply echo secular therapeutic practice but rather expresses an essential dimension of the call to confession of the church.

Yet pastoral care would be wrongly understood if it were thought to consist only of the assurance that the person will not be rejected or abandoned. Pastoral care is as well the active search for personal transformation. It is in the hope of such a transformation that a person comes to a pastor, who is therefore not merely a passive ear but also an agent (or co-agent) of transformation. This too is an essential aspect of the call to confession, which holds out the assurance not only that the one who comes will be neither betrayed nor rejected but also that dialogue characterized by trust and truthfulness will lead to liberation and growth. Pastoral care aims not only at awareness but at transformation, deliverance, and liberation. There is considerable difference among pastoral counselors over the degree to which this transformation is effected simply by the relationship of acceptance itself. For some this appears to be the full definition of pastoral care, while for others it is clear that positive "intervention" and wise counsel are essential aspects of the pastoral process. In my own view pastoral care is more than hearing, however attentive and evocative. It is also speaking, so it is active rather than passive. This would in any case follow from the full application of the model of confession to the practice of pastoral care.

The establishment of a pastoral relationship is the living out, with another person, of the essential characteristics of a call to confession. The initial stages of pastoral care correspond to this call in the building of a relationship of trust and acceptance oriented toward transformation.

C. The Diagnosis of Bondage

The act of confession is the disclosing of aspects of brokenness and bondage within the self that are normally hidden from view. This disclosure requires an environment of trust and acceptance, which is announced in the call to confession and established in the early stages of a pastoral relationship. It also requires the hope that this disclosure will not simply name this brokenness but will also transform it, bringing a greater measure of freedom and health, a promise likewise modeled by the call to confession and by the offer of help implicit in any therapeutic relationship.

The disclosure in view here is not the airing of incidental "lapses" or the enumerating of superficial symptoms sometimes associated with the term *sins*, but is the uncovering of more fundamental wounds and structures of brokenness. The symptoms (sins) are significant insofar as they trace the more fundamental structures or dynamics (sin). The analytical insights of modern psychotherapy, based on the work of Sigmund Freud, are characterized precisely by this establishing of procedures to elicit and interpret such symptoms in order to understand the more fundamental vicissitudes and structures, which are their cause.

Both psychotherapy and confession suppose that the first step toward human freedom and health is disclosing that which is hidden. Accordingly, a pastoral care informed by the wisdom of confession has good reason to welcome the assistance of analytical insight in this task.

It must be clear that the pastoral role in   *165*

confession, like the psychotherapeutic one, is more than a mere listening. It is a disciplined attention to and careful probing of the other's discourse. It is a listening that guides the speech of the other to more and more fundamental awareness and disclosure of his or her brokenness and bondage.

The attentiveness of pastoral listening is a concrete expression and avowal of the dignity and worth of the other. This dignity and worth is by no means conditional on some degree of wholeness but rather is that unconditional regard which mirrors the divine graciousness. Pastoral attention then conveys the conviction that no demonic power of the heart or of history can separate us from that love made manifest in Christ and made present in the pastor's attention.

The listening is also a probing. It is a guiding that seeks to penetrate the superficial and the illusory in the quest for truthfulness. This truthfulness is not possible apart from attentiveness. It cannot be the result of imposing metapsychological or theological theory on the density and complexity of actual human experience. But the quest for truthfulness may be guided by an understanding informed by analytical theory, and by theological reflection on the subterfuges by which bondage cloaks itself or weakness masquerades as strength.[4]

It is only insofar as the person who comes for counsel actually recognizes the concrete brokenness and peculiar patterns of bondage characteristic of his or her lived experience that confession becomes potentially liberating.

---

4. For a discussion of the relationship between theological and psychological understandings of human brokenness, see my "Human Brokenness: The Dialogue Between Theology and Psychotherapy," *Journal of Theology for Southern Africa* (January 1978), pp. 15-25.

Of course in some ways this process of "confession" is coextensive with life itself. Usually, the person can find the aid of friends and a caring community to be a sufficient framework within which to pursue this growth in self-awareness. But at times, when this process is blocked or when the skills for such reflection have not been developed or supported within the community, the assistance of a professional counselor may be of great help. Conversely, the pastoral counselor can by no means substitute for the permanent responsibility of persons to engage in this liberating reflection within the environment of the community. The pastoral counseling relationship, unlike the relationship to a caring community that regularly models this reflection in its liturgy and its life, is not permanent but temporary. Professional pastoral counseling ends when the person is prepared to make constructive use of aids provided by the community's life and worship for this continuing task of liberation. Recognizing the relationship between pastoral care and pastoral liturgy may help to strengthen the ties between the community and those set apart for this ministry, as well as to facilitate the transition into and out of the pastoral counseling relationship for the member of that community. Moreover the experience of pastoral counselors may be very important in forming liturgical actions that appropriately guide the continuing work of confession.

D. Transformation

One of the dangers to which both moralistic and analytical forms of counseling are prone is the fostering of an unhealthy self-preoccupation, which paralyzes rather than mobilizes and which isolates rather than leads to relationships of   *167* spontaneity and generosity. In the liturgical paradigm that should guide a pastoral form of counseling, this temptation is interdicted by the turn away from bondage (repentance) and in the turn toward freedom articulated in the prayer for pardon. Taken together these actions compose the practice of transformation.

Of course, there is much truth to the view that the process of becoming aware, of disclosing bondage and brokenness, is itself transforming. The motto of Freud, "Where id [the unconscious] was, there shall ego [consciousness] be," indicates a profound transformation in the situation of the self—the deliverance that light brings to a fearful darkness. For this reason many pastoral counselors content themselves with the work of confession as itself the beginning and the end of the liberating or therapeutic process.

But despite the attractiveness of the philosophical spirit that animates this identification of awareness with deliverance, it is not, I am convinced, adequate for a genuinely pastoral practice of counseling and care. Christian faith seeks not only to name the principalities and powers but to overthrow them, not only to name the demons but to cast them out. A pastoral care that exemplifies this faith will not be content to name or catalog the neuroses that dominate us but will seek to diminish their power over us and to aim at a more fundamental deliverance. All too often, identifying understanding with transformation results in a cherishing of neuroses (or "besetting sins" as these were once known) rather than renouncing them in the hope of greater freedom.

This resignation to and preoccupation with the forms of bondage and brokenness represents a failure of hope, but it is an essential

168

task of ministry to awaken and encourage hope. The gospel, which is the basis of all forms of ministry, exists not so that the world may be understood better but that it may be made better. It is this hope that is articulated in Marx's axiom that the task of philosophy is not only to understand the world but also to transform it. And this is an essential aspect of pastoral care: to nurture the hope and the yearning for transformation. Many persons, as William Lynch reminds us, have lost the capacity for hope. Pastoral care that knows something of prayer and of the prayer for pardon (deliverance) will seek to enable persons to articulate their most fundamental yearnings and hopes.[5] It is indeed only in the light of such hope that it is possible to see clearly the actuality of bondage and brokenness. Often our incapacity to see our chains is a result of our resignation to them. Persons cannot see the patterns of distortion in their lives with others if these patterns are merely self-evident—the way things are. But when these patterns are contrasted with the hope for other kinds of relationships and behavior it becomes possible to see them and to renounce them.

And it is with the renouncing, the turning away from patterns of destruction and diminishment, that transformation actually begins. To repent is not to repress but to transform. An important activity of pastoral care, then, is to assist persons to turn away from patterns of bondage and to devise patterns of freedom. In the medieval confessional this was the role of the "works of satisfaction." These works were all too often merely

---

5. For a discussion of some of the relationships between the "theology of hope" and pastoral care, see Charles V. Gerkin, *The Living Human Document* (Nashville: Abingdon Press, 1984), pp. 56-76.

"religious works" and had little or nothing to do with the actual brokenness and bondage of the individual. Yet the emphasis on such works was a clear recognition of the need to make concrete beginnings in the transformation of life. Thus Luther was quite right (as subsequent reforms in Catholicism have also acknowledged) that works of reconciliation with the neighbor, the family member, and others are of far greater value than candles and the repetition of prayers. It is in this connection, too, that O. Hobart Mowrer has identified restitution and reconciliation as essential work in the process of psychological healing.[6]

It is certainly *not* the task of the pastoral counselor to impose arbitrary "works" on the person who seeks help. Rather, the appropriate task is to help the person explore possible courses of action she or he may try out as a means of breaking patterns of bondage and of experimenting with behavior that better reflects liberation and healing. It is in this "trying out" of ways to unravel vicious cycles in relationships or attitudes that repentance takes form as a turning from the old and toward the new.

Pastoral care is necessary where the capacity for hope has been severely damaged or where one is no longer or not yet able to imagine new styles of attitudes, relationships, or behavior. In these situations, pastoral counseling will seek to reawaken hope and to strengthen the capacity to imagine and realize alternative styles of life. When the person is once again able to make use of the calls to hope and the assistance in transformation available in a committed community,

---

6. O. Hobart Mowrer, *The Crisis in Psychiatry and Religion* (Princeton: Van Nostrand Reinhold Co., 1961).

the role of the professional is superseded by that of the community. Whether in confession or in transformation, the pastoral counselor represents the community of faith and represents the need of all persons for the help of others. We cannot confess alone or transform ourselves alone. For this we need community. Pastoral care is the specific form of community we need to enable us to make use of the committed and caring community the church ought to be.

E. Beyond Adjustment

Secular therapies often aim at adjusting persons to the difficulties and stresses of life in urban, industrialized societies and their constituent nuclear families. Unquestionably this aim may be seen as merciful in that it seeks to diminish the pain persons experience under the social conditions in which they live.

But pastoral care that is informed by the liberating gospel cannot rest content with this aim of adjusting and accommodating—despite its (apparently) humanitarian and merciful character. In the light of the gospel, many of these social conditions must appear profoundly destructive to human dignity. Adjusting to them is then not a sign of health but of sickness. Many forms of psychological theory and practice are cut off from the kind of social awareness that can see these conditions as demonic. They thus have little choice but to seek adjustment to them. This can never be the case with a *pastoral* counseling and therapy rooted in the gospel. Nothing could be more fatal to the pastoral identity or character of our care than merely accommodating people to public structures of brokenness and bondage.

But to be liberated from social illusions   *171*

and from public forms of brokenness is to become even more vulnerable to the pain of the contradiction between what one hopes for and the reality one experiences. Pastoral care does not ease this pain although it may enable persons to understand it and to transform it into a constructive capacity for engaging and challenging these structures.

The aim of the liturgy of liberation is not merely to liberate persons but to enable them to become agents of liberation. Without this people are condemned to be only the objects and not the agents of "the forgiveness of sins." Indeed, apart from this movement toward preparing agents there can be no liberation. A major portion of human bondage is the destroying of the capacity for agency. Thus techniques of accommodation can never really be therapy (healing), but only palliatives. They relieve the distress while leaving the disease unchecked.

The aim of a truly *pastoral* care then is to enable persons to become agents of transformation in a world of brokenness and bondage. In this way, pastoral care will enable persons to take their place within the Body of Christ as the living representatives of God's mission of liberation and of God's ministry of healing.

The Liturgy of Liberation and the Sacrament of Penance

12

I n this book we have focused on the liturgical sequence of call to confession, confession, repentance, prayer for pardon, assurance, and absolution as it may be found in many churches of the Reformation. One of the questions that have divided Western Christianity since the time of the Reformation is that of the sacramental character of such an action. Although Luther very early argued against the sacramental character of marriage, ordination, confirmation, and unction, he retained for some time the view that penance should continue to be viewed as a sacrament.[1] Even when he ultimately concluded that it was not to be viewed in this way he insisted on its crucial importance. On the basis of the clarification of this "liturgy of liberation" I have proposed in these pages, it is appropriate that we should reopen the question of the sacramental character of this action. I believe that an evangelical understanding of the liturgy of liberation opens the way for renewed dialogue between Protestants and Catholics on this issue.

---

1. Luther, "Sacrament of Penance," pp. 21-22.

A. The Sacramental Character of the Forgiveness of Sins

Of course the question of the sacramental character of the confession and forgiveness of sins depends on the way we understand sacrament. Some Protestant communities completely reject this category as entailing unacceptable metaphysical confusions and magical abuses. Others adopt a more or less traditional view of sacrament and limit the sacramental actions to two: baptism and eucharist. Certainly this is not the place for an extended treatment of the question of the definition of sacrament, which would take into account the history of this category and the disputes surrounding it. Instead I will simply remark in what sense I believe it can be said that the confession and forgiveness of sins is a sacramental action, and in what sense an evangelical understanding of this sacrament may still vary from the traditional or even modern Roman Catholic views. This final chapter, then, is intended to suggest further dialogue among the churches.

1. The Command of Jesus

One characteristic of a sacrament that has been emphasized especially by Protestant theologians is that it is an action instituted by the clear command of Jesus. Thus the action of baptism appears to be instituted by the resurrected Jesus in Matthew 28:19, and the eucharist appears to be instituted by the words "Do this in remembrance of me," which are reported by Paul (I Cor. 11:24-25). It is noteworthy that the baptismal command is found only in Matthew and the eucharistic command only in I Corinthians (it is not found in any of the Gospel accounts—indeed there is no account of a last supper of bread and wine at all in the Gospel of John). Despite the scantness of reference to

174

an explicit command of Jesus in connection with these two sacraments, the whole weight of church tradition and the clear practice of the early Christian community confirms that these commands have generally been understood as binding upon the community of Jesus' followers.

Is there then a similar command that may be taken as instituting the action of the forgiveness of sins? Of this there can be no doubt. In addition to the many instances of Jesus exhorting his disciples to forgive their enemies (Matt. 18:21; Luke 6:27, 35), we encounter in the Gospel of Matthew the clear commission to forgive sins. On the first occasion this commission is directed to Peter (Matt. 16:19) in response to the confession of Jesus' messiahship. On the second occasion (Matt. 18:18), this commission is directed to *all* of Jesus' followers. But unlike the baptismal commission, the commission to forgive sins is not limited to Matthew's Gospel. It is the final commission of the risen Christ to his followers in the Gospel of John (20:20-23). Thus as an action instituted by the clear and express command and commission of Jesus the forgiveness of sins actually has a clearer foundation in the New Testament than either baptism or eucharist.

2. The Word of Promise

A further characteristic of sacramental action is that it is accompanied by the clear promise that in and through our action God also acts in such a way as to liberate and save. This promise of God to act through our action is what makes a sacrament "an outward and visible sign" (our action) of an "inward and spiritual grace" (God's action). In late medieval philosophy and theology, this was expressed by the theory that the work (our action) works (God's action) so that what is signified   *175* by the action is actually accomplished through that action. The Reformation sought to remove the magical associations that had accumulated around this theory by emphasizing the importance of faith on the part of the recipients of sacramental action. Nevertheless, the promise of God to act in and through our action was taken to be fundamental to the definition of sacrament.

The promise that God comes to us to liberate and save in and through the action of baptism is never explicit in the New Testament but it is implicit in the reflections of Paul on being "baptized into Christ" (Rom. 6:11–8:39). The same is true of the eucharistic action of breaking bread and drinking wine in the name of Jesus (I Cor. 11:17-34). But while the promise associated with baptism and eucharist is implicit and indirect, the promise associated with the forgiveness of sins is explicit and unequivocal.

In the first place, it is clear in a way that it is not for baptism and eucharist that our relationship with God actually depends on our participating in the act of forgiveness. In the Lord's Prayer we ask God to forgive us as we forgive others and to this Jesus adds the warning, "But if you do not forgive men their trespasses, neither will your Father forgive your trespasses" (Matt. 6:15).

But to this warning is added the promise that God will act in and through our action. To Peter Jesus says, "Whatever you bind on earth shall be bound in heaven, and whatever you loose on earth shall be loosed in heaven" (Matt. 16:19), and this promise is repeated to all the followers of Jesus in Matthew 18:18. In the Gospel of John, the risen Jesus promises his disciples: "If you forgive the sins of any, they are forgiven; if you retain the sins of any, they are retained" (John 20:23).

176 If a sacramental action is one that is instituted by Jesus, one that our relationship to

God depends on, and one in and through which God acts as we act, then the forgiveness of sins must be understood as such an action. Indeed, at every point its claim to this status is even clearer than is the case with baptism or eucharist. But there are other more general considerations concerning sacraments that contribute to the view that the forgiveness of sins may be understood as a sacramental action, and it is to these that we now turn.

3. *The Sign of the Action of God*

When we speak of an action as a sacrament we mean that it is an epitome of the whole action of God in Christ. Thus baptism is not merely one isolated act among others but rather epitomizes the way in which God as Spirit brings the dead to life and so confers that new life, which is both abundant and eternal. Similarly, the eucharist is an action that represents the reconciling work of God focused in the cross of Jesus and aiming at the messianic banquet and new creation.

In a similar way the forgiveness of sins may be viewed as an epitome of the liberating act of God, which aims at the freedom of the whole creation, through the Liberator-Messiah. Thus, as we saw in chapter 3, the activity of Jesus in healing and exorcism is focused and explained in the forgiveness of sins (Mark 2:1-12).

Paul is able to summarize the entire gospel as the justification of the ungodly. But this justification is nothing other than the forgiveness of sins, the liberation of people from bondage and brokenness, which are the presence and manifestation of sin.

The forgiveness of sins then is not an isolated act alongside a great many others, but is instead an epitome of the whole action of God in the person of the Christ, who is the Liberator. In   *177* the public performance of this action in our worship and in our life, we give public testimony of the whole work of God as Savior and Redeemer.

4. The Sign of the Action of the Church

The intelligible and regular action of the gathered people of God is normally referred to as liturgy. This liturgy represents the action of God and gives typical or paradigmatic expression to the imitation of and response to that action by the people of God. Thus in the liturgy, the community of faith discloses its identity and enacts or performs this identity in order to remind itself and testify to others what it means to be the people of this God. The many dimensions of this identity are articulated through the varied liturgies the community of faith enacts.

Some of these actions are more central than others, expressing more directly and concentratedly the identity of this people as the people of this God. These especially concentrated elements of liturgical life are called sacraments.[2] Thus the performance of baptism is a concentrated expression of the identity of the community as those who have passed from death into life on account of

---

2. I have attempted to work out some of the elements of a general theory of liturgical and sacramental action in more specific ways. See "On Ritual Knowledge" in *The Journal of Religion* 62 (April 1982): 111-27, as well as the articles, "Liturgy" and "Sacrament" in *The Encyclopedia of Religion*, ed. M. Eliade (New York: Macmillan Publishers, 1986). I have attempted also to clarify the ways liturgical action generates theological discourse in *Beyond Theism: A Grammar of God Language* (New York: Oxford University Press, 1985). These more philosophical and phenomenological reflections serve to indicate the methodological basis of the sort of reflection undertaken in *Life as Worship: Prayer and Praise in Jesus' Name* and in this book.

the prior grace or unconditional favor of God, and as those who have been commissioned to summon the rest of humanity into this new life. Similarly, the eucharistic action of the church represents the many ways this community participates in Christ (through memory, hope, and community with one another and the earth) as the reconciler of humanity with God.

We may also view the liturgical enactment of the forgiveness of sins in a similar way, for here is concentrated not only our identity as a people forgiven and so liberated by God in Christ but also our identity as a people commissioned to act as God acts: liberating the earth from brokenness and bondage. Our liturgical life as the announcement and enactment of this liberation is concentrated in the confession and forgiveness of sins. If, as Moltmann has contended, all Christian proclamation may be summarized in the liturgical pronouncement *ego te absolvo* (I forgive you), then the forgiveness of sins is the concentration of that ministry of the word, which constitutes our Christian identity. The forgiveness of sin is the sacramental form of the proclaiming of the word.

5. *The Sign of the Eschaton*

The term *sacrament* stems from the Latin translation of the Greek *mysterion* or "mystery." In the Jewish and early Christian literature of the first century, a "mystery" designated something that reveals or anticipates the expected consummation of the reign of God. Thus in Ephesians 5:32 marriage is called a mystery (or sacrament) in this sense: that the loving and faithful union of two distinct persons (originally strangers to each other) may be understood as representing the "marriage" of Christ and his people, and thus the eschatological joining of God with a humanity originally estranged from God but now united in eternal love and loyalty and joy. In this way the joining of two persons represents and anticipates the consummation of the divine promise of joyful union with all the earth.

In a similar way baptism is that act which anticipates the pouring out of the divine spirit over all the earth, transforming that life which is lived under the shadow of death into life abundant and eternal in a new heaven and new earth. Thus what appears as an isolated action performed for a single person (or group) is an anticipation (mystery) of the universal consummation of the promise of God in the end of all things. So too the eucharistic action of an individual community anticipates and symbolically displays the messianic banquet of universal reconciliation and joy.

The liturgy of liberation is a sacramental action in the same way. Through this liturgy the eschatological promise that God will heal the people of their sins, and so inaugurate the age of freedom from public as well as interior bondage is publicly enacted. This action anticipates the glorious liberty of the children of God for which the whole of creation yearns and toward which it aims (Rom. 8:19-22). In this way the public act of the people of God is a mystery or anticipation of the consummating of the divine action.

B. An Agenda for Protestant-Catholic Dialogue

The preceding discussion has demonstrated that there is a strong case to be made for understanding the forgiveness of sins as a sacramental action. Indeed in some respects the case for regarding the forgiveness of sins as a sacrament is even stronger than that for either baptism or eucharist. The way appears open for a fruitful dialogue between Protestant and Catholic churches concerning the place and importance of this action within the life of the community of faith.

Any such dialogue will have to seriously consider questions of the understanding and practice of this action whether or not it is taken to be a sacrament in the strict sense. Since I believe it is appropriate to regard the forgiveness of sins as a sacramental action, it is important to mention some of the ways an evangelical view of this action may differ from the understanding and practice of this sacrament in traditional and modern Catholic theology. Such a discussion has the aim of suggesting items for the agenda of Protestant-Catholic dialogue on this subject.

1. Grace and Faith

Medieval practice of the sacrament of penance (as this action was then known) was often characterized by a magical misunderstanding of the action. Against this misunderstanding it must be stressed that sacramental action is not the casting of a spell but the practicing of a paradigm.

Of considerable assistance in this regard is Luther's emphasis on the place of faith in the sacramental action. For Luther the faith of the hearer is essential to the efficacy of the pronouncement of absolution.[3] This is not to say that faith itself is the only action or that it is *the* decisive action. Faith is the response to the pronouncement of pardon, which is grounded in the words of assurance and anticipated in the call to confession. Thus, the primary action is the act of forgiveness, which awakens faith, which calls it into being. Yet apart from this faith, this hopeful and confident response, there can be no confession, no repentance, no yearning for pardon, no release from bondage and broken-

---

3. Luther, "Sacrament of Penance," pp. 11-15.　　　　*181*

ness. If we do not believe in the possibility of liberation we are unable even to see the magnitude or radicality of our bondage, still less to renounce it and turn toward freedom. Yet faith is by no means its own ground. It is a response to a word of promise and assurance that it does not produce. I cannot address *myself* with the word that interrupts my solitude with assurance and release.[4] I cannot be for myself both I and Thou. The word that awakens faith must come to me from another, and apart from such a word and deed there can be no liberation. But if that word remains external to me, if I do not rely on it, it cannot deliver me from my bondage or heal the wounds of my brokenness.

This dialectical relationship of gracious word and faithful hearing is clearly exhibited in the confession and forgiveness of sins. Indeed, by attending to this action, we may become clearer about the ways grace and faith interact in sacramental action generally, and so be assisted in purging the theory and practice of sacramental action from magical deformations.

2. Liturgy and Word

One of the limitations of Western medieval sacramental theory was its tendency to focus on an isolated moment in the liturgy as the sacramental moment par excellence. Thus the words "This is my body" or

---

4. So Luther writes, "Since by God's grace it is commanded of us to believe and to hope that our sins are forgiven how much more then ought you to believe it when God gives you a sign of it through another person," ibid., p. 14. And Bonhoeffer notes, "Self-forgiveness can never lead to a breach with sin; this can only be accomplished by the judging and pardoning Word of God himself," *Life Together*, p. 166.

"I baptize you in the name of the Father, the Son, and the Holy Spirit" or "I absolve you" were isolated from the liturgical sequence of which they were a part and so invested with an arcane and quasi-magical efficacy. Just as syllables, words, or phrases divested of context may become nonsense (try repeating the word *syllable* fifteen times), so isolating a sacramental formula such as *"Hoc est corpus meum"* may create an incantation, "hocus pocus" which will only be nonsense to the intelligent hearer. To be sure, this isolation may originally have answered to a genuine pastoral need: the desire to assure persons that despite all variations in detail the sacrament was properly performed if only the central formula had been uttered.

Whatever the pastoral exigencies that led to this isolation, its catastrophic consequences are clear in retrospect. This isolation must be countered by insisting that the sacramental action is the liturgical sequence as a whole and not an isolated moment within that sequence. This would bring Western sacramental theory more into conformity with the Orthodox understanding of sacrament, which has avoided both this isolation and the magical associations derivative from it by insisting on the sacramental character of the liturgy as a whole.

With respect to the forgiveness of sins, this would mean that the sacramental "act" is not the pronouncement of absolution alone but the entire sequence of actions: call to confession, confession, repentance, prayer for pardon, assurance, and absolution. It is this sequence as a whole that demonstrates or exhibits the liberation that is intended by the forgiveness of sins. It is this whole action of the people of God that is the outward and visible sign of the divine action and promise.

Insisting on the integrity of the sacramental sequence will not diminish but enhance the significance of the pronouncement of forgiveness, which is the aim and basis of the sequence as a whole. Confusion about the character of this action is demonstrated in the variety of names it has had: "confession," "penance," "reconciliation." But a consideration of the sequence as a whole and its basis in the biblical account makes clear that we are dealing here with the liturgy or sacrament of *forgiveness*, of deliverance from bondage and brokenness. Thus, the word of absolution, forgiveness, deliverance, or liberation is the focus of the action as a whole. Indeed the action as a whole is the indispensable context of this word, which articulates the liturgy's true meaning. Paradoxically, attention to the liturgical sequence as a whole gives greater prominence to absolution than a sacramental theory that isolates the formula only to speak of a sacrament of "penance."

Attention to the sequence as a whole further clarifies the dialectic of grace and faith. The gracious word of promise and deliverance (call to confession, assurance, absolution) is answered by the faithful response of confession, repentance, prayer for pardon. Only together as grace and faith, as word and hearing, as promise and trust is this action a truly sacramental action.

3. Priest and People

Attention to the liturgical act as a whole may also help to make clear that the sacramental action is the action of the whole people of God rather than the action of a priestly office separated from the people. One of the rallying cries of the sixteenth-century Reformation was the "priesthood of all believers." This cry was directed particularly against

184

the abuses of priestly prerogatives in the confessional. The Catholic reformation of the twentieth century associated with the Second Vatican Council has gone far in responding to the basic insight of the priesthood of believers, and subsequent Catholic theology has often called for further movement in this direction.

Attention to the liturgical action as a whole makes clear that the sacrament is performed not by one person or class of persons but by the people as a whole in the corporate exercise of priestly office.

Here it must be emphasized that the priesthood of all believers does not deny the priesthood of some believers but insists that all share in this priesthood. Unfortunately the cry "priesthood of *all* believers" has often only meant "the priesthood of *no* believers." In other words, in order to correct the abuse of authority of some persons, the authority and responsibility of all has been denied. This is catastrophic.

With respect to the forgiveness of sins it must be clear that *all* Christians have this authority and responsibility.[5] *All* are commissioned to bind and loose and to *all* is given the promise that in their action God acts. The denial by some Protestants that a mere human being has the power to forgive sins is a denial of the clear and unambiguous word of scripture.

Often this denial is accompanied by the pious assertion that I do not need a mediator between myself and God. In the extreme form in which this is normally

---

5. Thus the commission of Matthew 18:18 and John 20:23 is directed to "the followers" of Jesus in general. Luther insists, "The keys are yours and mine" ("Sacrament of Penance," p. 16), and Bonhoeffer maintains, "This commission is given to the whole congregation and the individual is called merely to exercise it for the congregation" (*Life Together*, p. 113).

understood it is utterly false. In the creation narrative we are told of the divine judgment that it is not good for man to be alone (Gen. 2:18). And the effect of Jesus' ministry is not to leave each of us alone before God but to place us each in relation to the neighbor. It is in this neighborly relationship that our priesthood consists, for our actions are to be modeled on the divine action—loving, healing, forgiving.

The true and evangelical meaning of the priesthood of all believers is the protest against usurping priestly responsibility by a particular group or class of Christians. While in a given situation one person may represent the priesthood of all the people, it is truly the priesthood of all that is thus modeled and displayed. If the leader of the liturgy pronounces forgiveness of sins this is not because *only* she or he may do so but rather to demonstrate that *all* may and must do so. The promise of efficacy is not made to a particular group or even to a liturgical action as such, but to any act of forgiveness by any Christian. The word of absolution uttered by one who represents the priestly office of the people of God is not more efficacious than the word or deed of the ordinary Christian. The difference between the liturgical forgiveness of sins and the liberating act or word of any Christian anywhere is not one of efficacy but one of corporate significance. The liturgy is the blueprint, but the act of the believer is the project itself. The blueprint is not more real than the house or garden of which it is the model.

All believers are commissioned to forgive sins. We attain clarity about what is involved in this authority and responsibility through the liturgy, which serves as a model, paradigm or blueprint for this action. The leader of the liturgy who pronounces forgiveness demonstrates the authority of all and of each. A priesthood that supplants or diminishes the priesthood of the believer cannot be a priesthood reflective of Christ, who commissions all to exercise this authority. In the legitimate exercise of priestly authority and responsibility, the believer acts toward the neighbor in such a way as to demonstrate the divine action. I cannot be my own priest—but any Christian may and must be priest to any other. That I must be addressed by another is represented in the liturgy by the word of call, assurance, and absolution. But this word also models my responsibility to address others with this same word of freedom. Thus the Christian is at one and the same time the recipient and the agent of the priestly word of forgiveness, and this double character is modeled in the liturgy of liberation.

4. Public and Private

Considering the sacramental character of the liturgy of liberation points us toward an emphasis on the public and corporate character of this action. In the medieval period, public or corporate confession and forgiveness was increasingly replaced by the private "confessional," which became the locus of the "sacrament of penance." It was in this situation that the word of absolution disappeared from the public liturgy to be hidden in the confines of the private confessional.[6]

An evangelical reappraisal of the sacramental character of the forgiveness of sins leads to a return to the corporate and public character of this sacramental action. The entire church practiced this as a corporate and public action throughout the early centuries. The

---

6. Thus Aquinas could maintain, "But such absolutions as are given in public are not sacramental, but are prayers for the remission of venial sins," *Summa Teologica*, pt. III, q. 84, art. 3.

Orthodox churches continue this practice in unbroken continuity with the early church. Indeed only in the Synod of Whitby in 664 was the public and corporate practice of forgiveness of sins finally subordinated to the private confessional in the West. A return to an emphasis on the public and corporate character of sacramental action would be an important step toward restoring the interconfessional and historical unity of the Body of Christ.

In this way as well the ecclesial character of sacramental action may come into clearer focus, thus correcting the privatism and individualism of Western conceptions of the forgiveness of sins. Moreover it is only in this way that the action can be truly sacramental as an "outward and visible sign" of the action of God. It is not the hidden and private action of the confessional but the public and corporate action of the liturgy that is genuinely sacramental.

If the corporate liturgical practice of the confession and forgiveness of sins is understood as the sacramental action in the proper and narrow sense, this will mean that ecclesial actions modeled on this sacrament may be understood as sacramental in a derivative sense. Thus, continuing the private confessional as well as the forms of individual or group pastoral care modeled on the confessional may be understood as elaborations and applications of the sacramental forgiveness of sins. But this should not detract from the importance of the individual acts performed by Christians, whose lives are formed by the forgiveness of sins. It is in the mission and ministry of unmasking illusion, of repudiating bondage, of solidarity with those who hunger and thirst for righteousness, of demonstrating confidence in the promise of God and in deeds of liberation, that the practice of confession and forgiveness

acquires its goal and becomes a true manifestation of the divine liberation for which we hope. The liturgical and corporate act is the model or blueprint of the reality enacted in our lives. To say that the liturgical act is sacramental or a sacrament means that it is this pattern. It exists only to serve the formation of liberated and liberating life-style.

5. Reconciliation or Liberation

Since Vatican II there have been a number of important developments in Roman Catholic reflection on the sacrament of penance. These reflections are represented, above all, by the work of Karl Rahner, which explores the historical roots of the practice of penance in the early centuries of the church[7] and proposes that this sacrament also be understood as a sacrament of reconciliation whereby persons are reunited in fellowship with the church.[8] On this view, sin is understood as having the effect of separating one from the holy church and, therefore, requiring penance and forgiveness in order to reconstitute the holiness of the fellowship of the forgiven. This view certainly accords quite well with early church theory and practice, and serves as a corrective against individualistic and magical misinterpretations that crept into the practice of the church during the centuries following the fall of the Roman Empire. In the North American realm, the emphasis has fallen so heavily on this revisionist view that the name "sacrament of penance"

---

7. Karl Rahner, *Theological Investigations*, v. XV. *Penance in the Early Church* (New York: Crossroads Publishing Co., 1982).

8. See Rahner's "Penance as an Additional Act of Reconciliation with the Church" in *Theological Investigations*, v. X (New York: Herder and Herder, 1973), pp. 125-49.

has largely been replaced by the term *sacrament of reconciliation.*[9]

Beyond question this change is a very promising one and requires careful and sympathetic attention from the side of Protestant theology. It is however necessary to mention some reservations that arise concerning the appropriateness of this new designation and understanding. In my own view, the action of confession and forgiveness of sins is primarily one of liberation rather than reconciliation. The sacramental action that displays reconciliation is the eucharist. Forgiveness is not only preparatory to participating in eucharistic fellowship but is an act of witness to the liberating power of God.

The ground of my reservation is the determination to adhere as closely as possible to the biblical norm. I do not share the view (widespread among many Protestants) that fourth-century church practice is axiomatic for liturgical practice (any more or less than twelfth-century practice, for example). Rather a theory of sacramental action needs to be tested, insofar as possible, against a biblical norm. Here it becomes clear that the command to forgive sins is *not* an adjunct to eucharistic action. It is, at least in important respects, an autonomous action.

The impact of this objection becomes more clear if we ask, What is the aim of the action? I do not believe this aim is adequately expressed by incorporation (or reincorporation) into the church. Speaking here of a sacrament of reconciliation only creates a new form of that ecclesio-centrism, which Protestants, at least in theory, have properly found to be a suspicious development. The aim of God's action is *not* to found the church but to transform heaven and earth, not to constitute a

---

9. E.g., see *The Rite of Penance: Commentaries, Background and Directories,* ed. Nathan Mitchell (Washington, D.C.: The Liturgical Conference, 1978).

Noah's ark of holiness but to save the world. This universal intent of the divine action is best articulated by speaking of a sacrament of liberation (from brokenness and bondage) rather than of a sacrament of reconciliation (to the church). The holiness of the church is not the absence of sin but its imitation of the divine liberating act. The church is holy because and insofar as it liberates people from bondage and brokenness, not because of the sinlessness of its members.

The aim of our action is not to unite people to the church but to liberate the world from bondage. In the "sacrament of liberation," we exhibit the responsibility and authority of the people of God to participate in this liberating action of God. To speak of a sacrament of reconciliation is to turn our attention away from the world as the domain of the divine action and the domain of our responsibility and authority. Instead we focus on ourselves (the church). In this way the missional structure and *raison d'être* of the church is subverted in favor of a deadly self-preoccupation.

The whole creation, says Paul, is groaning and yearning for the demonstration of the sovereign liberty and liberating authority of the newborn sons and daughters of God. We must not abandon *this* task for preoccupation with a mechanism to sustain ourselves as a "holy" people.

Thus I am persuaded that, despite the many advantages to be found in the transforming of the "sacrament of penance" into the "sacrament of reconciliation," an evangelical appraisal of the sacrament cannot be satisfied with this change. If we speak here of a sacrament, as I believe we should, then it is not of a sacrament of penance or of a sacrament of reconciliation but of the sacrament of liberation.

Conclusion

In these pages I have sought to indicate that a real basis for dialogue exists between Protestant and Catholic theology concerning the confession and forgiveness of sins. I believe that an evangelical understanding of this action provides the basis for reaffirming its sacramental character. At the same time I believe there remain important, indeed fundamental, points of divergence between such an evangelical view and both traditional and modern Catholic understanding and practice of this sacrament. I have sought only to discuss in a general way points of convergence and divergence rather than anticipate the results of such a dialogue. In any case it is to be hoped that a renewed ecumenical discussion of the confession and forgiveness of sins will not only be a sign of reconciliation between two groups of Christians, but will also aid us all in the common task of witnessing in liturgy and life to the divine promise and act of liberation.